Stage Lighting Controls

Ulf Sandström has participated in design of lighting control systems and training of theatre board operators over 10 years. He has also written a book on basic lighting techniques for TBV (Stockholm) and numerous articles for magazines in the music industry. He freelances around the world as a project manager, lighting designer, photographer and technical consultant.

Stage Lighting Controls

Ulf Sandström

(f)

Focal Press
An imprint of Butterworth-Heinemann
Linacre House, Jordan Hill, Oxford OX2 8DP
A division of Reed Educational & Professional Publishing Ltd

℞ A member of the Reed Elsevier plc group

OXFORD   BOSTON   JOHANNESBURG
MELBOURNE   NEW DELHI   SINGAPORE

First published 1997

British Library cataloguing in Publication data
A catalogue record for this book is available from the British Library

ISBN 0 240 51476 9

Library of Congress Cataloguing in Publication data
A catalogue record for this book is available from
the Library of Congress

Typeset by Keyword Typesetting Services Ltd, Wallington, Surrey, England
Printed and bound in Great Britain

PN
2091
E4
526
1997

Contents

Preface

Why even attempt to write a book about high tech equipment in a small sector of the entertainment technology industry? It would seem pretty hopeless to freeze the rapid development of new products in print, and who would read it? Every lighting console is delivered with a thick handbook explaining the characteristics of that product, right?

This may be true, but it's equally true that most of these handbooks are written by people who 'know' for people who hopefully 'know'. A handbook will explain individual features, but not where they have evolved from, what they may be called in other consoles and how they are intended to be used. As for the 'rapid development', the same basic principles for lighting control are being presented in new products every year. These principles will remain unchanged even if the methods for applying them are improved in every new product.

Why does this book exist?

I have enjoyed participating in the design of lighting control systems and board operator training for over a decade, and putting these systems to use in theatre, television and theme park applications. Throughout this time I have come across consoles that seemed to approach the concept of controlling lights in different and sometimes (to me) confusing ways, so I decided to investigate whether they were so different after all.

Even though new lighting products are presented every year the basic components of lighting such as intensity, focus, direction, colour and movement remain the same, but they can be applied in new or different ways, with more precision and (hopefully) in less time. This new technology is great when it serves an artistic purpose, but it can just as easily get in the way of a production because it doesn't behave the way you think it should. It is my hope that this book will help in understanding this technology, because I found that there are some general and basic concepts that will apply regardless of the specific lighting console being used.

What is this book about?

I picture a lighting design as a soundless concert. The lighting designer is the composer, the stage manager the conductor and the lighting console operator the musician. The lighting console is the control end of the 'light instrument', and can be played as crudely or passionately as any musical instrument. This book explains how the characteristics of a lighting console can be used to 'orchestrate' different light sources, colour-changing devices and moving lights. It gives a guide to how cues can be 'composed' and 'played' back in a show.

A less poetical way of describing it would be to say that this book explains the general principles of modern computerized lighting consoles and offers a condensed orientation to differences, possibilities and suitable working methods, regardless of brand. It also offers a historical perspective on the evolution of modern control systems, a guide to manufacturers and terms you will run into when dealing with modern lighting consoles.

Who is this book written for?

A book like this has a place in the library of every theatre, school or professional working in a situation involving lighting control. This is a guide to the basic control features of lighting control systems that can be used as a textbook, an encyclopaedia or a handbook by novices, operators, lighting designers, stage managers, electricians, technicians and any other production participants in a situation where lights are controlled. The material that is covered is of a technical nature, and the concepts that are described are not always simple (which is why I felt this book was necessary) but I have tried hard to use straightforward language that only assumes a very basic technological knowledge from the reader. And, of course, an interest in lighting controls.

How should this book be used?

Reading it from cover to cover would probably be a tedious affair even if it would provide the reader with a very broad understanding of the concepts of lighting control. I would recommend it as a textbook complement for general studies about lighting, as a handbook complement to product manuals and as a lighting control encyclopaedia.

Information disclaimer

I have made every possible effort to ensure that the information in this book is correct. Despite this, there may be errors somewhere in this book. Please let the editor know if you find any, I want this to be a perfect product.

Product disclaimer

I have tried to honour the products of different manufacturers equally, but I can assume that there are other equally competent manufacturers of lighting controls in addition to those represented in the examples and photos of this book. For practical reasons I have limited myself to the ten 'most prominent' or 'most actual' manufacturers at the time of writing the book (see Appendix 2). This may change and my recommendation is to contact the lighting industry trade associations in Appendix 1 and get their membership listings, which provide up-to-date information about most manufacturers in the industry. Find out more about these organizations in any case, because they can be very useful.

Acknowledgements

This book would not have been possible without the tremendous support it has received from manufacturers and other people in the business. There seems to have been a demand for a book of this kind because responses were immediate and supportive whoever I contacted. If I have omitted or forgotten anyone from this list, please accept my sincere apologies – I have carried my notes around the world with me as I have been writing between projects over a period of almost two years, and something may have been lost. I also want to thank my 'private' supporters, in the form of family, girlfriend and friends, for being so supportive despite most of this not making sense to you. I love you! Thanks!

In alphabetical order:

4 Star Lighting (US): Don Lawrence for a great afternoon firing up dusty old relics that have served on Broadway, and for providing information and material on these products.

ADB (Belgium): Dirk and Lucien Van Nieuwenheuysen and Thierry for being supportive and taking time to provide manuals, photos and proof-reading parts.

Anders Regnér, lighting designer (Sweden), for taking time to analyse a show he was operating from an Avolites console with a Celco Gold as a backup.

Anthony Isaacs, engineering consultant (UK), for taking time to discuss your involvement in the creation of the Thorn Q-File and the lighting industry at that time, and providing material and photos.

Arne Dahl, lighting designer (Sweden), for analysing one of your own designs for a show with a large moving lights component and Vari*Lites from a control point of view.

AVAB (Sweden): Kent Flood and Anders Ekvall for being supportive and taking time to proofread and provide input on some issues. Thanks to

Ralph Dahlberg for providing photos. I had most of the manuals, because I wrote them, but thanks for letting me use them.

Avolites (UK): Steve Warren and 'JB' for being supportive and taking the time to provide manuals, photos and proofreading parts.

Bash Theatrical Lighting, Inc. (US): Paul Kleissler and Ron Folwell for taking time to provide me with information from the point of view of a large rental company.

Camelont (Sweden): Magnus Annuell for an historical tour of the world of scrollers.

Celco (UK): Keith Dale and Mike Rothon for being supportive and taking the time to provide manuals, photos and proofreading parts.

Compulite (US): Fred Lindauer for material on the company, products and photos.

CP Sweden (Sweden): Joa Palmer for a guided tour of the Wholehog II, and Rickard Ahlstrand for material, manuals and photos.

Electronics Diversified (US): Paul Bennett for a historical perspective on the US market and photos.

ETC (US/UK): Fred Foster, Adrian Hicks, Kristine Hoevet and many more for being supportive and taking the time to help point me in different directions, providing manuals, photos and articles and proofreading parts. David Cunningham for historical background material to creating the first Light Palette.

Flying Pig Systems (UK): Tom Thorne and Nils Thorjussen for photos and information on the company background and the WholeHog II.

Francis Reid, theatrical consultant and lighting designer (UK), for discussing the project and providing a historical perspective on the importance of controls.

George Izenour and Jeff Milet for help with photos and information on early multi-scene presetting systems and thyratron valve dimmers.

High End (US): Bruce Jordahl for being supportive and taking the time to provide manuals, photos and discussing parts.

Jan Gouiedo, lighting designer and technical consultant (Sweden), for great support and valuable input on the material in general.

John Kliegl for digging up a photo of a Kliegl Performer.

Ken Billington, lighting designer (US), for giving me a lighting designer's perspective on tracking consoles.

Martin Overington, lighting designer (US), for taking time to explain your Avolites and Vari*Lite consoles at the Palladium in New York City, from a club lighting perspective.

Michael LoBue, lighting designer (US), for taking time to discuss different consoles from a lighting designer and operator's point of view.

Rosco/Entertainment Technology (US): Gordon Pearlman for providing historical insights to the LS-8, the Kliegl Performer and many other products that you have participated in engineering over the years.

Steve R. Terry at Production Arts (US), for being supportive and taking the time to point me in important directions, and for providing input on the material after proofreading.

Strand Lighting (UK/US): Tony Brown, Mike Cawte and Chris Winbank (UK), Björn Claesson (Sweden) and Peter Rogers (US) for being supportive and taking the time to help point me in different directions, providing manuals, photos and articles and proofreading parts.

Teatro (UK): Andy Collier for providing me with input on the project at an early stage.

Tim Hunter, lighting designer (US), for giving me a lighting designer's perspective on the applications of different control concepts.

Transtechnik (Germany): Hans Leiter for providing me with information about the history of Siemens, Transtechnik and theatre controls in Germany.

Vari*Lite (US): Tom Littrell for material and photos and taking time to discuss parts.

Vic Dobbs at Glantre Engineering (UK) for historical background material concerning the Thorn Q-file.

Zero 88: Richard Thornton-Brown for background information and photos of the Sirius.

Introduction to the basic elements of lighting control

A lighting rig is a general term for an assortment of equipment from different manufacturers, temporarily configured for a specific result conjured by a lighting designer: the sun will not shine through the window pane in the decor unless a *light source* has been chosen, tinted, focused and directed to create that effect; it won't set when 'night falls' unless it can be faded by a *dimmer*; and there has to be an operator who will initiate that change of intensity at the right moment. The operator will want to follow the action on stage, which means a *lighting console* is needed where lighting changes can be set up and *communicated* to the dimmers through a control signal, such as, for example, *DMX512*.

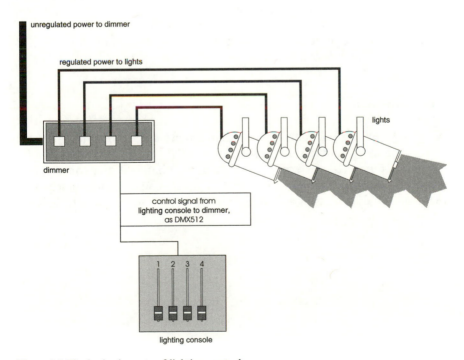

unregulated power to dimmer

regulated power to lights

lights

dimmer

control signal from
lighting console to dimmer,
as DMX512

1 2 3 4

lighting console

Figure 0.1 The basic elements of lighting control

Lighting consoles

The lighting console is the control interface of a lighting rig, from which lighting devices are controlled and 'looks' are stored into memories. Once this is done the lighting console can be 'played' to bring back the stored settings according to the action on stage. This book is about lighting consoles, how they operate and how they communicate to the lighting devices they control. *Part 1 – Background and Basics* provides a general understanding of lighting consoles. *Part 2 – General Console Features* provides an explanation of common control features, and *Part 5 – Troubleshooting* is a short guide for troubleshooting problems.

Lighting devices

The lighting devices are the actual instruments that produce light in some way. There are different types of conventional lights with optical systems and reflectors that are manually adjusted to produce different kinds of light beams that can be filtered through a colour gel to produce tinted light. The intensity of a conventional light is controlled by a dimmer that regulates the power to the light (see 'Dimmers'). There are special colour changing devices called scrollers (see 'Scrollers') for conventional lights, and there are 'intelligent fixtures' that allow remote control of movement, light, focus, direction and colour from the lighting console. These are often just called moving lights (See 'Moving lights').

Communication

A lighting console is a control panel that communicates to lighting devices such as dimmers, scrollers and moving lights. *Part 3 – Console Features for Specific Lighting Devices* explains how these are handled in a console, and *Part 4 – Communication* explains how a lighting console communicates to these and other devices in an entertainment lighting environment.

Part 1 – Background and Basics

Introduction

One of the easiest ways to see similarities and differences in various approaches to lighting control is to understand where each concept originated from. A modern lighting console can be very impressive with its high tech appearance and multiple screens when compared to the gigantic mechanical switchboards from the early 1900s, but those systems were considered just as ingenious in their time. Much has happened and much has not; the basic control concepts of the early systems remain the same but modern consoles are much more powerful and flexible, allowing several thousands of channels to be successfully controlled from a small console.

Chapter 1 describes 'The evolution of lighting control' from a control perspective, providing a thorough background to 'where' modern control concepts come from.

Chapter 2 condenses the concepts in Chapter 1 and provides four general categories into which most modern consoles fit, even though these aren't strict boundaries due to a constant crossbreeding between different sectors of the lighting industry.

Chapter 3 is a generic description of 'what a modern console consists of', with references to how different features relate to specific chapters and parts of this book.

Chapter 4 looks into the most fundamental rule that applies to every control channel that is addressed from more than one function in a console: should it interact on a 'highest or latest takes precedence' basis with the other functions of the console?

1   The evolution of lighting control

This chapter looks at the control of stage lighting from a historical perspective, highlighting factors that have played an important role in the shaping of today's control systems. The next chapter ('What kinds of lighting consoles are there?') is a condensed view of these functions in modern boards.

Why bother with history?

An idea about why features were invented can help in understanding them, because even if new boards are presented every year, most of the basic functions have been around for decades. Early dimming techniques had limitations that were explored in different control methods, and most of these traditions and terminologies have been passed on to modern boards. Every new technological advance such as computerization, moving lights or networking has added more functions and terminologies to the old.

Sunlight and fire

Early outdoor amphitheatres were built so the evening sun would provide a natural light, and open fires in the form of torches or oil lamps have been used in theatres for hundreds of years.

Candlelight

Early 'controlled' stage lighting consisted of candles, over which cans would be lowered, producing a dimming effect. In later and more sophisticated systems they could be mounted on a vertical reflector located on the sides of the stage, and 'dimmed' by rotating the reflector to control the amount of light reflected on to the stage.

Figure 1.1 Vertical candle reflectors (Courtesy Drottningholms Teatermuseum, photo Bengt Wanselius)

NOTE: Drottningholmsteatern is a uniquely preserved eighteenth century wooden theatre in Stockholm, Sweden, that still uses vertical candle reflectors.

Gaslight

1800 brought gaslamps into the theatre, providing higher intensities of light than candles. These light sources were 'dimmed' with mechanically controlled valves regulating the flame.

NOTE: An excellent book about antique lighting techniques is *Lighting in the Theatre* by Gösta M. Bergman, written for The Stockholm Studies in Theatrical History. Published by Rowman and Littlefield, New Jersey, ISBN 0-87471-602-0.

Electric light

In 1879 Edison invented the filament lamp, which gave a brighter light than gas, oil or candles without the smoke or potential fire risk. The same year a permanent lighting installation was made in the California Theatre of San Francisco. In Europe, the first theatre to announce electrical lighting 'throughout' a performance was the Savoy Theatre of London in 1881, with six controlled generators. Gas installations were gradually replaced by electrical installations, but the same year the French Opera House was still using a gas installation of 960 gas jets with 88 control valves – the equivalent of an 88 dimmer system! (source: Frederick Bentham, *The Art of Stage Lighting*, Pitman).

Resistance dimming

The principle of the first dimmers was to place a variable electric resistance in line with the lamp. Full resistance meant no light at all, and no resistance meant full light. Resistance dimmers were load sensitive, which meant they could only handle the load they were designed for. If, for example, a smaller load was attached (a lower wattage lamp) the dimmer would not be capable of dimming it to a complete blackout, but this could be corrected by adding a 'ghost load' along with the lamp. A disadvantage of resistance dimmers was that they consumed power whether the load was dimmed or not, which resulted in a waste of power transformed into heat.

Liquid resistance dimmers

One of the first resistance dimmers consisted of two electrodes submerged in a partially conducting liquid (salt water). By separating the electrodes more liquid resistance was introduced into the circuit, resulting in a dimming of the lamps.

NOTE: When the Royal Shakespeare Company made The Aldwych their London home in 1960 a liquid dimmer installation from 1905 was still in use.

First single-scene boards with groups

Since liquid dimmers (for practical reasons) were located in the basement of a theatre, solutions for remote controlling them had to be created. The electrodes were controlled from wires, tracking over long distances and connected to regulator wheels in a large 'lightboard'.

Each dimmer was controlled by a separate regulator wheel. Several wheels were shafted together to a master wheel capable of dimming the whole group at once; this was called a group master. Lights that were used simultaneously (for example, footlights) were usually grouped to regulator wheels controlled by the same group master. In case there were several groups like this, there would be a Grand Master wheel, capable of controlling all groups simultaneously. This was what was called a single-scene board (only one control 'handle' per dimmer). There were tracker wire regulators for up to 120 dimmers.

Figure 1.2 Tracker wire regulator from 1940 (Courtesy ADB)

Wirewound resistance dimmers

Another solution was to introduce a varying length of wire (coil) between the electrodes. This could be done in two ways:

(a) A slider construction, where one electrode would be slid against the side of a wire coil, thereby varying the resistance. These dimmers were often controlled manually by sliding the control handle of the electrode over the coil.
(b) A plate construction with several wire coils of varying resistance mounted to a plate. By shifting from coil to coil on that plate, different resistances were introduced into the circuit.

Several resistance plates could be mounted together in direct-operated manual boards with one lever for each dimmer and a master lever to bring all up or down. These were usually located close to the stage, with fuses and switches all incorporated into a large 'switchboard' that was run by several operators. There were portable versions with around ten dimmer channels mounted together in a box called 'road boards' (sometimes also called 'piano boards' due to the resemblance of the box to an upright piano).

Figure 1.3 Slider dimmer (Junior 8 slider dimmer, courtesy Strand Lighting)

Figure 1.4 Resistance 'road board' (Century portable switchboard, courtesy Strand Lighting)

Road boards were popular in the United States (especially on Broadway) well into the 1970s, which helped shape the concept of modern tracking consoles (see 'A third philosophy – tracking consoles', p 23).

Early lighting companies

Siemens Bros of England (later Germany), and Clemançon of France (1828) were among the first companies involved in theatre lighting (among other things), but soon dedicated companies were started. Kliegl Bros was founded in 1896 in New York, Strand (UK) in 1924 and ADB (Belgium) in 1920.

Mechanical auto-transformer dimmers

In the early 1920s a new type of dimmer was designed that solved the drawbacks of resistance dimmers, allowing varying loads and smooth fading, without unnecessary power consumption resulting in heat transmission. Instead of introducing a resistance between the power and the lamp, the lamp was fed from a mechanical arm that 'tapped' a varying voltage from a

Figure 1.5 Eighty-channel manual direct handle switchboard from Liverpool (Grand Master, courtesy Strand Lighting)

track on a transformer coil. The electrical qualities of a transformer made this design self-regulating, 'automatically' matching the power to the load.

Since the arm had to be moved mechanically, these dimmers (often referred to as 'Bordonis') adapted perfectly into existing European tracker wire installations for resistance dimmers. Especially in Germany, the policy of subsidizing larger theatres played an important role for these costly but refined remote-controlled installations. In the rest of Europe and the United States, less expensive and more rudimentary installations still consisted of manually operated dimmer handle boards with everything assembled into a gigantic switchboard such as the Strand Grand Master system that was built for up to 80 channels, and run by several operators (Figure 1.5).

Electromechanical remote control

Up to this point only tracker wires, or direct mechanical links, had been used to remote control dimmers. Remote control was desirable because dimmers could be located close to the stage in whatever area was available and the controls could be brought to a separate position where the operator(s) could view the actions on stage.

In 1934 Strand Lighting came up with an electromechanical solution for remote controlling dimmer handles by a magnetic clutch arrangement that made it possible to move the handles with an electrical impulse. The legendary Strand engineer and lighting designer, Frederick Bentham, designed a control interface called the Light Console, based on a modified all-electric organ console. Bentham's philosophy was 'you have ten fingers and two feet', and the nature of the organ console fitted perfectly into his idea of 'playing' the lights. These are some important concepts that were introduced with the Light Console:

(a) *Group memories with rate control*
The Light Console was similar to a tracking wire regulator from a control point of view, because it was a single-scene board with group masters. The 'news' was that dimmer channels could be selected or deselected to different group masters using the organ 'stop tabs', similar to the way in which different organ pipes are selected to be played. The keys were used for moving the selected groups of lights up or down, and the organ volume (swell) pedal provided a speed control for the fades.

(b) *Integrated colour control*
The remote control of colour wheels mounted on lights was incorporated into the console. A set of keys was used for preselecting colours, and the change was initiated by one of the organ foot pedals.

Around 14 installations were made, a 120-channel installation in the Royal Opera House of Covent Garden used a Light Console between 1946 and 1964.

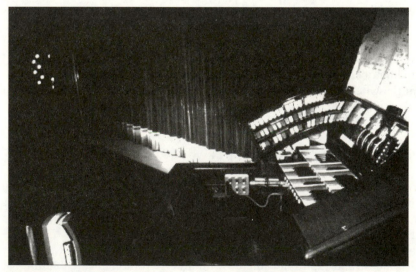

Figure 1.6 Group fading lighting console with organ keyboard as front end (Light Console, courtesy Strand Lighting)

First all-electric dimmers

The next advance that made new control philosophies possible was electrically controlled dimmers. One of the first all-electric dimmers was the saturable reactor dimmer, which employed a technique similar to the mechanical auto-transformer dimmers. A transformer coil was placed in series with the lamp load and a small electrical DC current was induced to saturate the iron core of the transformer, which would 'choke' the power to the lamp. A very small current (250 mA) was sufficient to control a power flow of up to 3000 W.

The last action principle

An electrically controlled dimmer would go to a blackout or full light when the control signal was removed, but a mechanical dimmer would stay on the level it was last set to until moved again. This property of a mechanical dimmer is the origin of the last action principle, also called latest takes precedence (LTP). This principle is used in modern control systems as a general description for something that stays where last set until moved again.

Multi-scene presetting

The all-electric dimmer made new control solutions possible, because an electrical control voltage could be generated from more than one control in a board before it was sent to the dimmer. This made it possible to have two or more control levers for each channel, and while one was 'live', different levels could be preset on the other levers. Instead of moving every single channel to a new level, a crossfade could be done by fading between the master for the first levers for all channels to the master controlling the settings of the second levers. Each new set of levers for a channel was called a new scene, in which a look could be preset. A board with several scenes was called a multi-scene presetting board. The concept of crossfading between preset scenes is still used in manual controls today, and is the concept of preset-oriented cue playbacks in modern lighting consoles.

In 1933 General Electric made a truly massive installation of all-electric dimmers at Radio City Music Hall in New York City. An impressive total of 314 saturable reactor dimmers was installed. It was a multi-presetting system with five levers per channel plus a rehearsal lever.

In 1947 a 44-channel multi-scene presetting system (Figure 1.7) was developed for Yale University Theatre complete with a new approach to all-electric dimming. The controls consisted of a main console with rehearsal

Figure 1.7 Early multi-presetting console with ten miniature presetting panels (courtesy Special Collections, Lehigh Univ. Information Resources – George C. Izenour Papers)

and master levers for each channel and a large wing with miniature controls for ten presetting scenes. The dimmers were electronic twin valves which achieved a dimming effect by switching on/off at a high speed (60 times per second), 'chopping' up the AC sine waveform into 'parts' that produced a variable RMS (medium) voltage instead of limiting the current by introducing a 'resistance' into the circuit or 'transforming' it. These valves were also called 'thyratrons' and although the concept worked, the valves were both sensitive and expensive. In 1959 the same principle was reapplied with solid state 'valves' and is still the prevailing dimming method (see 'The solid state dimmer – a landmark!', p. 14).

The manufacturing rights to this system were acquired by Strand Century, and this type of manual multi-scene presetting control was popular in the United States for many years.

Load patching

A multi-scene presetting board was 'manageable' for a single operator up to around 50 board channels. In the United States this was compensated by using, for example, 50 dimmers to which several hundred lighting circuits

Figure 1.8 Load patch from 600 circuits to 200 dimmers 6–12 kW (Courtesy Strand Lighting)

could be routed with a load patch. This created a central role for load patching in the United States while European theatres preferred installations with large numbers of smaller dimmers, which led to other control solutions such as group fading. Nowadays most lighting is done on a 'dimmer per load' basis, but the philosophy of 'patching' several light dimmers to one board channel lives on in the soft patch facility of modern boards and is frequently used in concert lighting consoles (see 'Patching').

Group fading

Presetting provided the advantage of allowing scenes to be set up in advance, but an elaborate side-effect was that all channels had to be preset for each change, including those that remained on the same level. This was time consuming and limited the possibilities of making quick scenic changes or controlling large amounts or channels due to the sheer size of the presetting panels.

Figure 1.9 Hundred-channel manual three-scene group fading system (Threeset, courtesy Strand Lighting)

A flexible solution that made it possible to achieve several changes without having to expend a whole 'preset' was to assign certain channels in each scene to separate group masters (with a switch) and to fade between these subset 'groups'. Group fading was flexible and lent itself to controlling large numbers of channels since only channels moving to new levels were affected in a change (see Figure 2.4).

Group faders were soon incorporated in two or three scene presetting boards providing a flexible mix of two methods. Minor changes could be achieved by fading between group masters and larger changes by crossfading to a completely new preset scene. This is the concept of modern group fading cue playbacks, where group fades are called move fades and preset scene fades are called crossfades.

NOTE: In 1947 the Broadway success 'Oklahoma' hit London's West End and started a new era of musicals, boosting business for the lighting industry.

The solid state dimmer – a landmark!

In 1959 dimming technology was blessed with the solid state silicon controlled rectifier (SCR), which achieved dimming using the same principle as the thyratron valve dimmers from the mid-1940s, but the solid state SCR was less expensive, more effective and more stable. SCRs are also called thyristors which are used in pairs and are sometimes built together into a triac.

The SCR dimmer revolutionized the concept of lighting control because it brought low wattage dimmers to an economical level where there was no reason for load patching because dimmer-per-load configurations could be used instead. Nowadays this type of dimmer is still the prevailing technology even if there are concepts being developed around other kinds of solid state devices such as transistors.

Memory in lighting controls

From the very start most manufacturers were looking for ways of controlling large amounts of control channels, allowing quick transitions between previously plotted level settings. The multi-scene presetting boards and group fading concepts were manual approaches to this, and the memory tabs in the 1934 Light Console qualified as a limited 'memory' system, but up to this point no manufacturer had completely solved the question of how to allow reliable 'instant recording' and 'random access' to memorized level settings.

There were systems that stored level readings to punch cards, like the Memocard from the Danish inventor Grosman, but these had to be 'read' sequentially to access the memories. There were also pin-matrix systems, where 'memories' could be set up manually for a number of submasters by sticking coloured pins corresponding to intensities into a matrix panel, but this would hardly qualify as 'instant recording'. One of the first systems to provide reliable 'instant recording' and 'random access' to memories was initiated by requirements from the television lighting industry.

Television lighting was slightly different to theatre lighting: most television shows were 'one-offs' with little preplanning, that could involve sudden changes 'out of script' and demanded access to individual controls and groups for random changes. The BBC (the UK public broadcasting channel), which started in 1936, had pioneered TV lighting techniques from early on. In the mid-1960s the BBC were going from black and white television to colour, which channelled a demand for more sophisticated lighting controls.

The first 'true' memory board – a landmark!

The BBC asked Thorn Electric (UK), who manufactured dimmers at the time, to manufacture a memory playback system to their specifications. The Q-File was presented in 1966, following three main design rules that are just as valid in modern memory consoles.

1. *You should be able to reach any control sitting at the desk*
An operator should be able to access any individual control sitting at the desk and following the action in the studio. In the Q-File all controls for 390 channels and 100 cues were available to the operator from a control panel with an area of less than 2 square feet (which meant channel faders were eliminated).

2. *You only have two hands*
Frederick Bentham's Light Console, based on an electric organ, was designed from the philosophy 'you have ten fingers and two feet', which meant a fair amount of dexterity was required of the operator. The controls of the Q-File were made simple, requiring little more than pressing a key or moving a fader to initiate memory fades.

3. *You should be able to do whatever you want at any moment*
The improvised nature of television lighting, with little preplanning, required facilities for 'stacking' looks by adding and subtracting memories, and then 'unfolding' whatever had been set up into a new memory.

Most of the basic approaches to memory control of lights in the Q-File remain unchanged in modern lighting consoles:

(a) *Channel control*
The channel faders were replaced by a single servo fader that would move automatically to the level of any channel selected from a digital keypad. The keypad consisted of vertical rows of 'digital' keys (ones, tens and hundreds), where keys lit up displaying the number of the selected channel. This solution provided a mechanical representation of both channel (keys) and level (servo fader) with direct access to make changes. This is the predecessor to keypad channel control in modern boards.

(b) *Studio and preset 'stores'*
The Q-File had a 'live' studio store and a 'blind' preset store which were the electronic equivalents of two manual channel scenes. The channel keypad could be set to work in either of these, and the settings could be stored into any of the 100 memories for random access. Working in the preset store made 'blind' plotting and memorizing possible. Calling up a memory to the studio store would replace all 'live' lights with the settings of that memory, similar to fading in a preset scene. Modern consoles have similar electronic stores for 'blind' and 'live' plotting.

(c) *Visual feedback*
Recognizing the need for visual feedback to the operator with the channel key lights and the servo fader, the Q-File also had a dimmer action display

unit with incandescent (28 V) lamps simulating the dimmer output of a memory. Modern consoles use monitors to display information.

(d) *Rate playbacks*

The 'fade engine' between the preset and studio store can be compared to a 'conveyor belt' to which memories were 'dumped' in the preset store, and transported to the studio store at the speed of the conveyor belt. This speed was set by two speed levers, one for the up-fading channels and one for the down-fading channels. This is the electronic equivalent of a multiple scene playback with infinite group faders in the form of memories.

One of the vital features required by the improvised nature of television lighting at the time was the possibility of 'piling' different memories onto the playback depending on the actions in the studio, and then 'untying' everything with a transition to one memory.

- *Crossfades*

All levels in the stage store could be replaced with new settings from the preset store, which is similar to fading between two preset scenes in a manual board. For example, a 'day scene' could be active in the stage store, and a 'night scene' could be loaded to the preset store, after which a crossfade between the two in 2 minutes could be initiated.

- *Move fades*

A memory could be faded in without replacing the whole contents of the stage store, which is similar to the group fading principle of a manual board. For example, if the 'night scene' was lit, the memories containing 'streetlights' and 'full moon' could be faded in, adding those channels to the 'night scene'.

A memory could also be 'minus faded' from the output, fading out only channels common to that memory. For example, the 'night scene' could be set to fade out, leaving the 'streetlights' and 'full moon' intact.

These combinations made it possible to add and subtract memories live, with the advantage of being able to 'unfold' everything with a crossfade to a new memory at any point. For example, the 'streetlights' and 'full moon' could be crossfaded to a completely different 'day scene'.

- *Fades within fades*

In boards with two or three playbacks, one could be running a crossfade of, for example, 5 minutes for a 'sunset' while the other was used for faster transitions. This possibility of simultaneous fades with different time bases was also called 'fades within fades'. This is addressed in different ways in modern consoles, some having multiple playbacks and some allowing 'fades within fades' in the same playback.

Figure 1.10 First 'instant recording and random access' memory board (Q-File)

(e) *Manual crossfaders*
There were separate faders for making possible a manual crossfade between the studio and preset stores, as in a two-scene manual preset board. The rate playbacks did not eliminate the need for 'hands-on' manually controlled crossfades, something which is recognized in most modern consoles.

(f) *Submasters*
The need for individual masters to control, for example, follow spots was addressed by a section of pin-matrix submasters. In modern consoles submasters are a standard component, but they are programmable.

Why memory boards?

Even though the Q-File was designed for television it also became popular in the theatre, but it was eventually replaced by the Strand Modular Memory System (MMS) (1974), which offered improved theatre functionality at a lower price. Memory boards introduced a new level of artistic possibilities in lighting control. There are five important advantages of memory control:

(a) *Retrievable levels*
Being able to store a lighting look was a great advantage. A lighting look could be stored and accessed with a single command instead of being recreated manually by balancing every single channel to a predefined level. Any previously recorded look could be recalled, edited to perfection and updated, allowing a new, more precise control over the lighting design.

(b) *Unlimited 'scenes'*
Since memories could be faded into a 'live' store replacing earlier memories, transitions were possible between an almost unlimited number of preset scenes.

(c) *Artistic consistency*
Being able to arrange the predetermined order in which these looks were to be played back, with individual fade times for each transition, guaranteed that even a complex show could provide the same result night after night, and allowed the operator to concentrate on timing the fades perfectly with the actions on stage.

(d) *Channel scenes unnecessary*
Since all memories could be stored from the same set of channel faders, only one set was required, which reduced the size of a board drastically, but the concept of selecting channels from a keypad and setting levels with a general level device made possible controls without channel faders. The MMS introduced an 'incremental encoder' for setting levels in the form of a wheel, which remains a popular level device since it never has to be matched to a level like the servo fader of the Q-file.

(e) *First command syntax*
In the first memory consoles, channels could only be accessed one by one, but in later models there were functions for adding and subtracting several channels or memories in a calculator style creating different methods for entering commands (see 'Command syntaxes' in Chapter 6).

Computers and lighting controls

Systems like the Q-File and the Strand MMS provided memory control of levels through computer technology in its earliest form, without processors or software. The Q-File memory system consisted of an elegant control panel connected to four six-foot-high racks where over 10 000 transistors and 15 000 diodes were assembled and hardwired to provide diode transistor logic. In the late 1960s Digital Equipment was manufacturing standard minicomputers that could be adapted to virtually any control requiring a central computer. Pretty soon it was obvious that a memory lighting system built around a computer could provide new advantages:

(a) *Software and updates*
If a computer is used to handle information, an instruction has to be written for how the computer should do this; this is called software. This can be a great advantage, because the functions of a computer system can be updated by rewriting the software and downloading it to the same system again. This means the functions of a memory console can be improved without changing the hardware.

(b) *Hardware*
The software is run on a 'hardware' platform which is the mechanical, physical side of a computer. This consists roughly of a short-term memory (called RAM) to keep the current show in, and a processor that follows the instructions of the software to direct information between inputs and outputs. The keys and faders of the board provide information to the processor that can be computed and output to the dimmers (as DMX512 or Ethernet in a modern board). The processor can also provide exact information about channels, levels and ongoing fades (etc.) in displays or monitors.

(c) *Long-term memory storage*
Many of the early memory boards could only hold one show in 'memory' at a time. By using a long-term memory storage system such as a diskette several shows can be stored and retrieved to the same console.

The first computer board on Broadway

One of the first computerized theatre lighting consoles was built by a company called Electronics Diversified in 1967. The LS-8 was a $100 000 system for 125 channels with a memory capacity of 100 cues (16kbyte core memory!) that was based on the principles of a multi-scene preset board. Every channel was set up to create a 'look' that was stored into a memory that could be faded between a 'blind' and a 'live' electronic 'scene' in the form of a crossfading cue playback. Since this allowed far more 'presets' than a manual multiscene board, this was also called an 'infinite preset' console. The LS-8 was the first computer board on Broadway, and was used for 'Chorus Line' at the Schubert Theatre. This board is now on display in the Boston Computer Museum as one of the first applications of minicomputer technology.

Figure 1.11 First computer console on Broadway (LS8, courtesy Electronics Diversified)

The industry expands

During the late 1970s and early 1980s more manufacturers were getting involved in computerized theatre lighting controls based on standard computers like the minicomputers from Digital Equipment, or proprietary concepts based on industrial processors. In the United States Strand and Kliegl were joined by Colortran, EDI and eventually ETC (to name a few), while in Europe ADB, Strand and Siemens were joined by newcomers AVAB (Sweden), Compulite (Israel) and Transtechnik (Germany).

Microprocessors and touring consoles

Thanks to new microprocessor technology manufacturers could fit the whole computer 'rack' into a small console, making it possible to produce smaller, cheaper and even more powerful systems.

In 1978 AVAB presented an incredibly compact console for 96 channels, complete with displays and a pin-matrix backup in a Zero Haliburton alu-

Figure 1.12 Microprocessor-based 96-channel touring memory console with pin-matrix backup masters (2001, courtesy AVAB)

minium briefcase. The system was designed for touring theatres but was used also for concert lighting by, for example, Supertramp and Pink Floyd.

In 1979 the 96 channel Kliegl Performer was launched incorporating a monitor and tape station into a 17 kg unit. The Kliegl Performer brought prices down from $50 000 to around $10 000 and was a popular touring console in the United States for many years.

Two control 'philosophies' so far

Up to this point two control philosophies were being applied in different larger theatre consoles:

Figure 1.13 Touring memory console, 17 kg with monitor and tape station (Kliegl Performer, courtesy John Kliegl)

- The preset-oriented consoles (like the LS-8) were 'infinite preset' versions of the manual multi-presetting boards, replacing the physical presetting scenes with cross-fading preset-memories.
- The group fading consoles (like the Q-File) were 'infinite group' versions of the manual two-scene group fading boards, replacing the physical group masters with move fading-group memories.

In 1980 AVAB launched a large-capacity preset-oriented system for 1000 channels (Viking), with voice synthesis that could 'read' cue texts to the operator, servo-controlled wheels providing 'tactile feedback' and an acoustic modem for remote servicing (Figure 1.14).

In 1977 Strand launched a large-capacity group fading system for 1000 channels (Lightboard) with a special group fading 'palette' panel and direct keys addressing various kinds of transitions between memories in the spirit of the Q-File (Figure 1.15).

A third philosophy – tracking consoles

In the United States most computer consoles were preset oriented, which meant shows were stored and played back as a series of isolated events

Figure 1.14 Early 1000-channel preset-oriented memory console (Viking, courtesy AVAB)

Figure 1.15 Early 1000-channel group fading memory console (Lightboard, courtesy Strand Lighting)

Figure 1.16 The first tracking console (Light Palette, courtesy Strand Lighting)

involving levels for all channels. Broadway lighting designers were still used
to designing shows with single-scene resistance road boards where a dimmer
handle would remain where it was last set until moved to a new level
(according to the last action principle). This meant shows were designed
as a sequence of partial moves related to each other involving only channels
changing to a new level.

The tracking concept was designed around this principle, which meant
only channels with a new level were stored in cues, and channels which
remained on the same level tracked through subsequent cues from where
they were last set. Strand presented the first tracking console in 1980 (Light
Palette) taking the Broadway market by storm with this 'electronic road
board' (Figure 1.16).

The following are general features introduced with the Light Palette, and
are just as valid in modern tracking consoles (see also 'Cue playbacks').

(a) *Tracking cue sheet*
The concept of a single-scene playback with 'tracking' levels was designed
for editing a sequential lighting design as a linear 'flow' from the first to the
last cue. To make editing simple, all cues could be looked at in a 'cue sheet'
in which channels changing levels were displayed differently to channels
'tracking' their levels from previous cues. The tracked levels were displayed
on the black and white screens in 'half' intensity, whereas today a colour
coding system is used to distinguish stored levels from tracking levels.

(b) *Single-scene playback*

The playback panel had eight physical and close to a hundred virtual faders that addressed the same playback scene. Each time a new cue was started it was assigned to one of the eight faders so it could be manually overridden during the fade, and if more than eight cues were in progress simultaneously the virtual faders were used. Each fader was the equivalent of a group master in a single-scene manual board, which meant several memories could run simultaneously as long as they didn't address the same channels.

For example, a fade with 'sunlight' on channel 1 at full in 6 minutes could be started as cue 1, then cue 2 was started after 1 minute with a 'daylight scene' in 30 seconds, but no new level for channel 1. Since there was no new level for channel 1, the 'sunlight' would continue to fade in the remaining fade time (5 min) and the 'daylight scene' would finish in the 30 seconds.

(c) *'Tracking' fades*

All fades were move fades, which affected only channels stored to that memory, allowing other channels to continue earlier fades as in the example above. If cues were played out of order, the computer would recalculate 'missed' moves and reproduce the correct end result on stage (see 'Cue playbacks').

(d) *Multipart cues*

When three operators operated six road boards they could achieve six simultaneous fades with completely different rates. This was implemented as multipart cues, which could be divided into six 'parts' with individual fade and delay times (see 'Cue fade times', p. 91).

(e) *Command line syntax*

The command syntax was designed so that all functions could be expressed as a command line where no action would take place on stage until an enter key was stroked (in a typical computer fashion). When the designer of the Light Palette visited a prototype (used for 'Beatlemania in Chicago') the way the lighting designer communicated with the board operator inspired him to adapt the command syntax to simulate the spoken commands. 'Go to cue 16' was translated into a key called 'GOTO' followed by cue number 16 and 'ENTER' (see 'Command syntaxes', p. 74).

(f) *First soft patch*

Even though this is not a specific tracking feature, the Light Palette was the first system with a soft patch, which meant that dimmer numbers could be reorganized to channel numbers that made sense to the way the lights were used (see 'Patching').

(g) *Designer station*

The system also introduced a 'designers' remote screen' to display the operations in the board to the lighting designer in a different location in the
theatre. This is a commonplace feature in different large theatre consoles
nowadays.

Memory boards for concert lighting

Up to this point concert lighting was lagging behind theatre and television
controls in sophistication. Most concert lighting was done with pin-matrix
mastering consoles that would have 24 submasters that could control one
lighting look each, set up with diode pins representing different levels in
a pin matrix. This was an inflexible and elaborate way of achieving
'memories', but also uncomplicated and straightforward. A lighting design
consisted of these 24 different 'looks' that could be combined and played
live according to the action on stage. (Modern concert lighting is still played
from submasters, but the functions of the submasters are far more
powerful.)

In 1981 Celco (UK) launched a 90-channel console (Gamma, Figure 1.17)
with 30 memory submasters, which was one of the first 'live' consoles for
concert lighting using 'theatre memory technology'. The following features
were introduced:

(a) *Memories and submaster pages*

Looks could be set up with a scene of channel faders and stored into the
submasters. If more than 30 looks were required, a new 'page' with 30 more
memories could be downloaded to the same masters.

(b) *On-board displays instead of monitors*

Each submaster had an eight-character display to show the 'name' of the
memory allocated to that master (for example, 'reddrums') which eliminated
the need for a monitor and provided the information right next to each
fader.

(c) *A sequenced effect option*

A list of memories could be assigned to a special sequence master and run as
a continuous effect which was a pretty spectacular feature in those days.

Memory controls all the way...

In 1987 Zero 88 (UK) brought the power of larger 'live consoles' to smaller
venues in the form of a 24-channel console (Sirius, Figure 1.18) with mem-

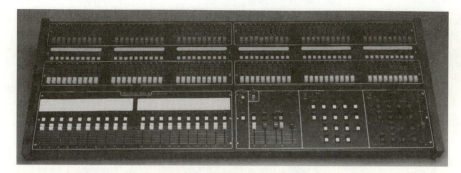

Figure 1.17 Early submaster memory live console (Gamma, courtesy Celco)

ories, fade times, effects and submasters at a new low-level price just over £1000. Memories were plotted with channel faders that could double as a manual two-scene presetting board, which made the concept extremely versatile and popular with schools, clubs, rental companies and other smaller venues. Nowadays many other manufacturers also offer amazing functionality in smaller boards at a low cost.

Figure 1.18 Sirius 24 (courtesy Zero 88)

DMX512 – a communications landmark!

Up to this point the only real standard for communication between lighting consoles and dimmers was the *de facto* 0–10 V standard of early analogue control, which requires multicore cables (see Chapter 16, Limitations of analogue control). Several multiplexing protocols were being used to communicate intensities for hundreds of dimmer channels in a single cable but the equipment of one manufacturer was rarely able to 'speak' to the equipment of another (see *Part 4 – Communication*).

In 1986 representatives of the lighting industry united at a USITT (United States Institute for Theater Technology) conference and agreed on the outlines of a specification for a standardized digital lighting control protocol. This meant a lighting console from any manufacturer would be able to control dimmers from any other manufacturer with little or no trouble using the same type of cable and connectors (see 'Analogue Control and DMX512').

Moving lights and scrollers

At the point of standardizing DMX512 several things were happening that would affect lighting design and consoles in a major way.

In the theatres the main component of a lighting design was conventional lights, but a new kind of colour changer was becoming popular, replacing antique 'colour wheels' which consisted of a large disc that could be rotated to place different gels in the front of a fixture. This new solution was a box with a 'roll' of gels that was mounted in front of an instrument that could 'scroll' to one of 11 different filters (see 'Scrollers').

Moving lights were being used in different ways. Some larger theatre houses were using remote-controlled yokes for high precision repositioning of lighting instruments that couldn't be reached between acts. At the same time companies like Vari*Lite and Morpheus (US) were using moving lights as a vital component in concert lighting. These companies practically dominated this market segment for many years manufacturing advanced, fast and wonderful moving yoke systems that were used mostly for larger concert venues to create complex light shows.

In the late 1980s two things happened:

1. Effect lights using a mirror to reposition the light beam (instead of moving the whole fixture) that had originally been designed for disco lighting (scanners), were also becoming popular for concert lighting.
2. The new DMX standard protocol was being implemented in scrollers and moving lights, allowing conventional lights and moving lights to be integrated in standard (DMX) systems.

Figure 1.19 The first Vari*Lite moving fixture (VL1, photo by Lewis Lee, courtesy Vari*Lite, Inc. All rights reserved)

In 1989 High End Systems (US) presented the first moving mirror unit aimed directly at the touring market. It was called Intellabeam and was fitted with DMX in 1991. Fifty units went on tour with Dire Straits shortly after, and a new era of moving lights had begun.

Moving functions in consoles

Today moving lights are a standard component in concert lighting, and theatre applications are steadily increasing. The instruments have recently become very sophisticated, and a single unit may have over 30 different control parameters, which has affected the requirements of the boards

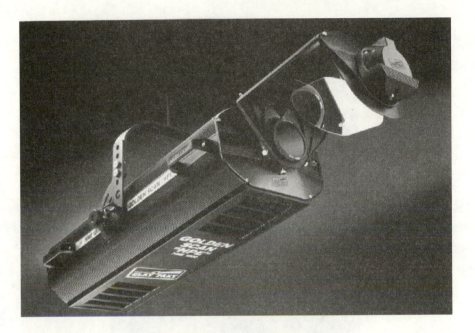

Figure 1.20 Moving mirror unit (Golden Scan, courtesy Clay Paky)

Figure 1.21 Theatre high-precision moving yoke (Auto Focus, courtesy AVAB)

Figure 1.22 Early moving light console (Animator, courtesy Compulite)

used to control them, and is a cause of steady development of new functions (see 'Moving lights').

In 1992 the first dedicated moving light consoles were launched with fixture libraries containing special control features for specific instruments, treating each fixture as 'one unit' instead of a number of control channels. Nowadays most consoles support moving lights to a certain extent, but there are still specific moving light consoles (see 'What kinds of consoles are there?').

Ethernet and networking

DMX solved how lighting consoles could communicate show data to dimmers, but it wasn't really designed for controlling moving lights or interconnecting lighting consoles with other show equipment. Recently a new way of interconnecting lighting equipment has emerged, allowing video signals, dimmer feedback, DMX data, MIDI and other show control data to be distributed in a single cable. An existing industry standard called Ethernet is used for this (see Chapter 17).

Where are we now?

This is where the history chapter ends. At the time of writing, new moving lights are evolving and most consoles are busy catching up with the complexity of these instruments by adding new features to simplify their use. Most larger consoles are adding networking features and Ethernet connectors and trade associations are working to standardize. Dimmers are still variations of the first solid state dimmer. There will probably be more advances in the use of transistors for different dimming methods that may produce a new generation of smaller and maybe more electrically 'quiet' dimmers. Conventional lights are becoming more effective with new approaches like the Source Four series etc., and lighting controls for conventional lights seem to have reached a certain point of 'stability' where most products are pretty good, and hopefully the expensive ones are better still.

2 What kinds of lighting consoles are there?

Most consoles are designed with a specific lighting situation in mind, with functions that are 'normally' required for that situation and a terminology 'expected' by users in that situation. There are four main categories of consoles:

- manual desks for low-end applications
- 'live' consoles for concert lighting
- 'theatre' consoles for 'playback'-oriented lighting
- moving light consoles

A certain crossbreeding has led to a point were functions and terminologies are being mixed in consoles of either category. Therefore it is more accurate to speak of hybrids such as, for example, a 'live console with manual facilities', a 'moving lights console with support for conventional lights' or a 'theatre console with support for moving lights'.

The playing factor of a console

The 'playing' factor of a console depends on functions that allow improvisation and quick access to 'riding' the controls of individual instruments. This usually means that physical controls like channel faders, submasters and bump keys are main features. This factor is important for 'live' lighting situations where the performance may include unforeseen variations, with little preproduction time and where the console operator and the lighting designer are often the same person. Consoles with a high 'playing' factor are often used for concert, club and television lighting.

The playback capacity of a console

Some consoles are designed so that a lighting designer can create a complex series of sequential lighting changes that can be operated from a GO button, guaranteeing that the design will 'live in the memory of the console' with the

option of depending as little as possible on the abilities of a specific operator. This means cue playbacks are among the main features, and usually
multiple monitors are supported to allow extensive editing and viewing of
large amounts of channels. Consoles with a high 'playback' capacity are
often used for theatre, musical theatre and theme park lighting.

The concept of manual desks

Chapter 1 explains the evolution of manual controls from the early tracking
regulators to multi-scene presetting and group fading controls prior to memory consoles. The following is a condensed résumé of the most important
principles of manual desks, which also apply to equivalent functions in
memory consoles.

Scenes

A single-scene manual desk (Figure 2.1) has at least one fader per channel
and maybe a master fader to fade all proportionally to zero. Every fader will
stay where it was last set until moved to a new position, and although this
may seem evident it is the most basic application of the famous last action
principle (also called LTP, as in latest takes precedence).

Presetting

Adding a second set of faders (scene B) (Figure 2.2) for the same channels
and another master fader will create a 'two-scene preset desk'. While one
scene is being output by 'scene A' a new scene can be set up 'blind' (master

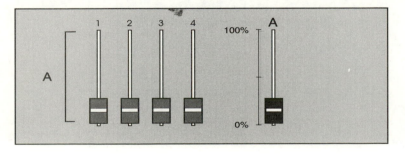

Figure 2.1 Single-scene manual desk

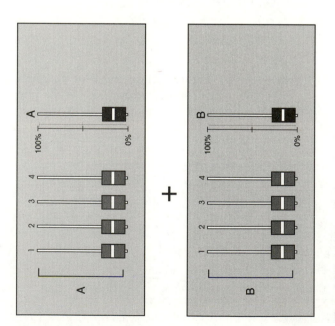

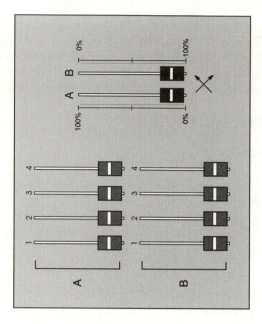

Figure 2.2 Two-scene manual preset desk

down) in 'scene B' and a 'crossfade' can be done by fading out the 'live' scene (master A) and fading in the preset scene (master B). This way an unlimited number of scenes can be preset and crossfaded with only two scenes. Usually one of the masters will be inverted in this kind of console so that both faders can be moved simultaneously during changes forming a 'crossfader' pair. Two-scene presetting is the most common type of manual control today, and is usually found in very small systems (6–12 channels) or as a manual component in a memory console.

Multi-scene presetting

When quick transitions are required more preset scenes can (Figure 2.3) be added to allow presetting several cues in advance. Nowadays manual multi-scene consoles are unusual because electronic 'scenes' in the form of memories that can be played back from submasters or cue playbacks offer the same advantages (and more).

Group faders

By allowing channels in each scene to be assigned to 'sub-scenes' in the form of group masters (with switches) (Figure 2.4), several transitions can be made without having to expend a whole preset scene for each. The concept of fading group memories without replacing the whole contents of a scene is used in memory consoles for transitions between cues in group fading and tracking cue playbacks.

Split and dipless crossfades

A linear crossfade between two masters that have 'split' (individual) control over one memory will each provide a 'dip' for channels that remain at the same level in both memories when both masters are half way (since no master is over 50% and as a result no channel can be over 50%). This dip can be avoided by fading in the incoming preset earlier than the outgoing (Figure 2.5).

Since this dip often isn't desirable for transitions in a cue playback, most modern consoles can 'look' at the incoming cue and 'keep' channels not changing at their current level during the fade. This is called a 'dipless' crossfade. Nowadays all memory consoles have dipless cue playbacks and only some manual two-scene desks still have split crossfaders (Figure 2.6).

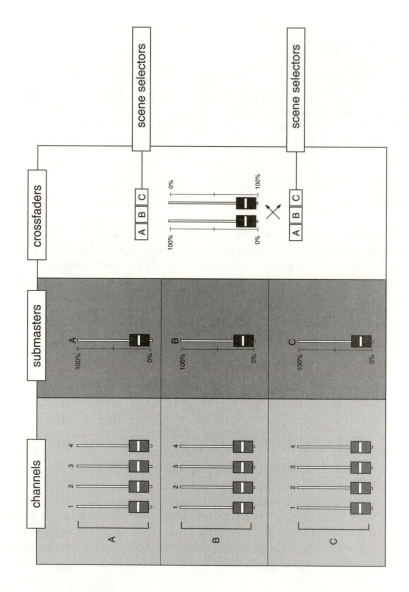

Figure 2.3 Multi-preset console with three scenes

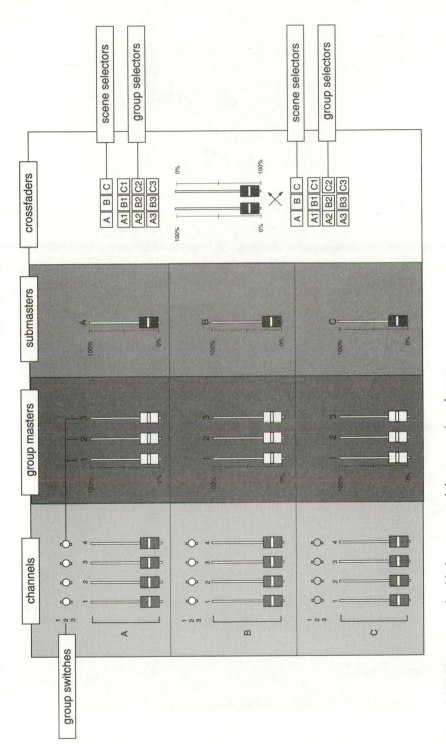

Figure 2.4 Multi-preset console with three scenes and three groups in each scene

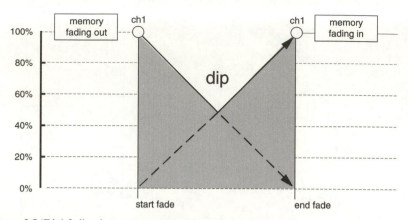

Figure 2.5 'Dip' fading between two memories

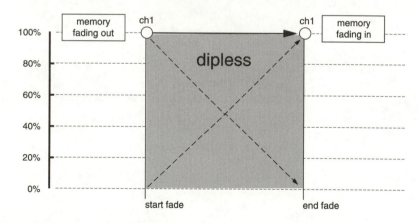

Figure 2.6 'Dipless' crossfade between two memories

Grand Master

With the possibility of several scenes adding to the same output and sub-controls of each scene in the form of group faders and submasters, a master control is required that can bring all intensities proportionally to zero without changing individual settings. This is called a Grand Master.

Blackout function

A blackout key is similar to a Grand Master in that it will bring all intensities to zero without affecting individual settings, but it is a momentary switch. It is often called BO (black out) or DBO (dead black out).

The concept of 'live' consoles

'Live' consoles are designed for situations where a high 'playing' factor is required, such as in concert lighting. The reason these consoles are called 'live' desks is not that theatre is 'dead', but that concert lighting can be much less predictable, with improvisations 'out of the script' where the operator needs to ride the controls during each performance.

Usually these consoles are designed so that the hardware provides a guide to the control features. There are a lot of manual 'handles' to pull for individual instruments, and direct keys for selecting 'palettes' of functions that can be thrown in for 'busking' a show. Because there are physical limitations to the amount of handles (for example, channel faders) a console can have, patching several dimmers to each channel is a common procedure in concert lighting since large groups of lights are often used simultaneously anyhow. Because live consoles are frequently used for touring they usually have alphanumeric keyboards for text input, and other accessories incorporated into the console, and most of the operator information is usually provided with on-board displays instead of monitors.

Originally these consoles are a continuation of the pin-matrix mastering consoles that had multiple submasters controlling different 'preset scenes', except that the pin matrix has been replaced by extensive memory functions. A show is often run fading from one submaster to the next, following the action on stage.

Support for moving lights

Nowadays the moving light component in concert lighting is high, and while 'conventional' live consoles may be used together with a separate moving light console, most incorporate advanced moving light support as an option for shows where only one console is used for both conventional lights and moving lights.

General features

The following is a summary of general characteristics that live consoles are usually designed around (in no apparent order). They are not rules, but provide a guide to important 'live' features.

- Plenty of control handles for individual instruments.
- Often several lights that are used simultaneously are patched to a limited amount of console channels, to have direct 'handles' for each lighting component.

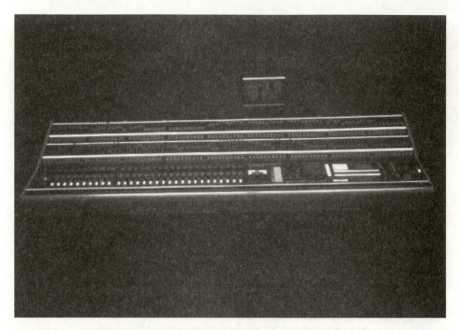

Figure 2.7 Large submaster-oriented live console with support for moving lights (QM Diamond II, courtesy Avolites)

- A show usually has to be patched before it is run.
- Plenty of submasters, which are the main playbacks.
- Each submaster can usually run either memories or effects.
- Cue playbacks may exist in complement to submasters.
- Extensive effects with functions for improvising to musical beats per second.
- A terminology of 'song'-oriented features coming from the concert lighting industry (each song is a small 'act' that can be played back out of order with other songs).
- More on-board displays and fewer monitors.
- Multiple DMX outputs to support different lines of moving lights and dimmers.
- Often support for moving lights.
- Desks can often be linked, and have sound/time code inputs for integrating light functions with interactive components of a show.

The concept of theatre 'playback' consoles

These consoles are designed to be used in situations where a high 'playback' factor is required, such as in theatre and musical theatre lighting. Complex

Figure 2.8 Large live console based on a group fading concept (Aviator, courtesy Celco)

transitions and lighting states can be stored allowing the option of not depending on the individual abilities of an operator. There are still functions for interacting with the playback features because often the operator is expected to exercise timing skills and to rebalance levels as necessary during performances (especially in repertoire theatres and opera houses). Sometimes these consoles are just called 'theatre consoles', which belies the fact that they are used also for theme parks, television lighting and other applications where the playback functionality is just as useful.

Different playback 'concepts'

Almost all theatre consoles have submasters that are used for mixing lighting groups into memories or controlling 'specials' during a performance, but the concept for editing and playing back cues is usually designed around one of three control philosophies. The end result of either method may be indistinguishable to the operator, but the methods of getting there are different. How each concept evolved is described in Chapter 1 and how this affects editing and playing back cues is described in Chapter 8; the following is a summary of all three.

(a) *Preset-oriented*

A preset-oriented playback 'thinks' in terms of a lighting composition 'broken down into individual states' that are crossfaded from a 'blind' store to a 'live' store similar to a multi-scene manual console. A console may have several cue playbacks, operating individually on a highest takes precedence basis.

NOTE: Some of the first computer consoles (such as the LS-8, see Chapter 1) were preset-oriented because it was a natural way of incorporating the functionality of a multi-scene board in a memory console. Today many theatre consoles are still preset-oriented.

(b) *Group fading*

A group fading playback 'thinks' in terms of a lighting composition 'broken down into individual states' *and* 'simultaneous groups fading transparently (move fades) in the same playback' like a manual console with multiple group faders. A console may have several cue playbacks that operate either together as group faders or individually on a highest takes precedence basis.

NOTE: The first memory boards (such as the Q-File, see Chapter 1) were group fading concepts to allow improvised transitions between memories in a single cue playback. Today group fades are a general concept in some theatre consoles and an optional feature in others.

(c) *Tracking*

A tracking playback is a group fading concept with special editing functions for playback situations with a 'totally linear composition' in mind, and the 'sequential flow' from cue to cue is central. These playbacks have both physical and 'virtual' faders, for simultaneous group fades within the same playback scene on a last action basis in much the same way that multiple operators would fade lights with direct handles in early resistance road boards.

NOTE: The first tracking console was launched in 1978 (the Strand Light Palette, see Chapter 1) and subsequent versions continued to build on this philosophy. In modern Strand consoles tracking functionality is a user-selectable option in the software. ETC launched a console line in 1992 (Obsession) that adopted most of the Light Palette's tracking concepts.

'Theatre style' channel control

The hardware of theatre consoles rarely reflects the complexity of a console, because many of the 'live' handles have moved into the software. For example, physical channel faders are rarely found except in systems aiming at the theatrical segment of the 'live' market or combined live/playback situations such as television lighting. Instead channels are usually accessed from a channel keypad in a calculator style. There are three dominant methods by which channels are addressed, called command syntaxes (see 'Channels'). The main difference between these is whether actions affect the live output directly or an enter key needs to be stroked first.

Does it really matter?

Different concepts for theatre consoles exist (and will continue to exist) partly because they are suited for certain situations, but mainly because local industries stay true to the type of system they have 'grown up with'. While every new console is expected to do 'exactly what the old one did', it is also requested that all the 'best features' of the 'other' systems be incorporated. Over the years this has led to most consoles compensating the advantages of the 'other' concepts. For example, tracking consoles have a cue-only recording function that is equivalent to a crossfading 'snapshot' cue, while preset-oriented systems have a record track function that will allow the same kind of editing through multiple cues as a tracking system (etc.).

The following illustrate three ways of looking at it from a lighting designer's point of view. In all three cases larger theatrical productions are involved, and the console operator is a different person to the designer.

- Ken Billington (US), a renowned lighting designer involved in everything from Broadway musicals and theatre to industrial shows, will use a tracking console in almost any situation, because he knows he will be able to do exactly what he has in mind and can 'walk any operator through the programming' if necessary since he is in full control of the command syntax traditionally used in tracking consoles. He also prefers thinking of a design as a continuous 'flow' from the first cue to the last.
- Tim Hunter (US), another renowned lighting designer involved in everything from Broadway musicals, dance and theatre to industrial shows, will choose which console to use after deciding what his design will require from a control point of view. It may be a subtle design with no moving lights, or a multilayered light movement where lights are active players. There is also the question of what the operator is used to and how the show is to be run once the design is done.

- Francis Reid (UK) is one of the pioneer theatre consultants and lighting designers who has both experienced and had an active part in the evolution of modern lighting control systems. To him, it was important to choose a console that would allow a certain kind of design many years ago, but these days most high-end systems are equally capable when it comes to controlling conventional lights.

Fixed installations

Many theatre houses have fixed installations that remain from ten to fifteen years, hoping to accommodate the needs of any performance set up in that theatre during this period. Therefore theatre consoles often have a very high data handling capacity and extensive editing functions to accommodate different situations. They are also often part of a fixed distribution net for control data accommodating fully tracking backup systems, designers' remote stations and dimmer status monitoring from the console.

Support for moving lights

Nowadays the moving light component in theatre lighting can vary from nothing at all to a major part. While theatre desks for conventional lights are sometimes used together with a moving light console, there is a tendency to incorporate both into one console for situations where only a few units need to be integrated into a show. The hybrids of today are usually theatre consoles with support for moving lights or possibilities to interact with moving light consoles.

General features

This is a summary of general characteristics that theatre consoles are usually designed around (in no apparent order). They are not rules, but provide a guide to important 'theatre' features.

- Mostly 'theatre style' channel control from keypad.
- One of three command syntaxes.
- One of three playback concepts.
- Theatres often have dimmer-per-load installations and may have a permanent inhouse patch set up in the console.
- Fixed installations with designer remote stations.
- Networking capacity to distribute show data within a theatre.
- Remote focusing units for stage electricians.

- Extensive printing functions to document plays.
- Cue playbacks are the main playbacks; there may be several.
- Manual and rate controls for interacting with playback features.
- Submasters are a complement to cue playbacks.
- Effect features are not as central as in 'live' consoles.
- A terminology of 'cue list'-oriented features coming from the theatre industry.
- Extensive editing capacity for large shows.
- Less on-board displays and more monitors.
- Multiple DMX outputs to support different lines of moving lights and dimmers.
- Support for moving lights to a varying extent.
- Functions for integrating backup systems that track the main system through a show.

The concept of moving light consoles

As Chapter 1 indicated, moving light consoles are the latest addition to lighting controls. In the early 1990s several concepts for controlling moving lights were launched, such as the Sapphire (Avolites), the Navigator (Celco), the Animator (Compulite) the Wholehog (Flying Pig Systems) and the Status Cue (High End).

Figure 2.9 Large theatre console with support for moving lights (Vision, courtesy ADB)

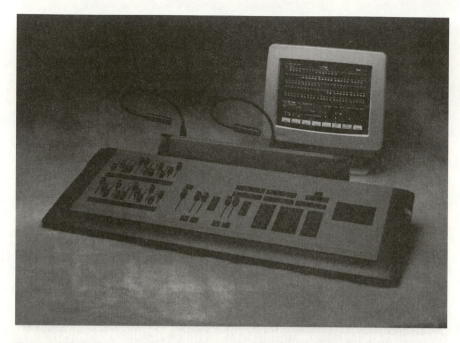

Figure 2.10 Mid-sized preset-oriented theatre console (Express, courtesy ETC)

Figure 2.11 Large theatre console with support for moving lights (Panther, courtesy AVAB)

Controlling moving lights can be very time consuming, because some fixtures have over 30 control parameters that each need to be programmed in three dimensions and tagged with different fade times in order to produce 'multi-coloured beams, dancing in time with the music'. Moving consoles recognize this and provide hardware and software features that speed up the

Figure 2.12 Tracking theatre console with support for moving lights (Obsession, courtesy ETC)

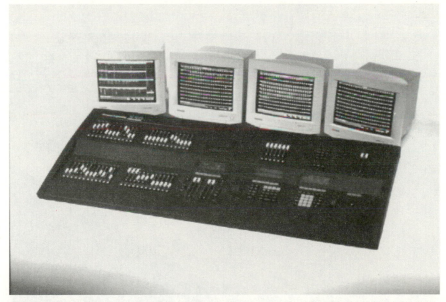

Figure 2.13 Large group fading (or tracking) theatre console with support for moving lights (Strand 520, courtesy Strand Lighting)

Figure 2.14 Large theatre console with support for moving lights (Prisma, courtesy Transtechnik)

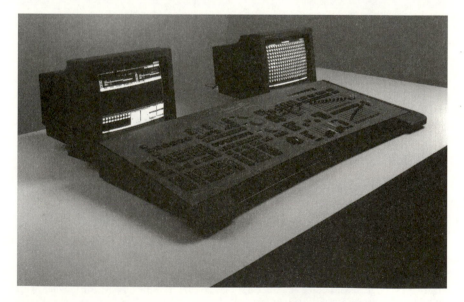

Figure 2.15 Large theatre console with support for moving lights (Ovation, courtesy Compulite)

programming of a show. How moving lights are controlled is described in Chapter 14.

Support for conventional lights

Even though most of the dedicated moving light consoles were used as complements to 'conventional' consoles in the beginning, they usually support conventional lights too. The reason is that moving lights may be controlled from a dedicated separate console with a separate operator if moving lights are a main component of a show, but there are shows where conventional lights are such a small component that they may as well be incorporated into the moving console. Since moving consoles often act together with conventional consoles, they are usually linked to these consoles (or the other way around).

General features

This is a summary of general characteristics that moving light consoles are usually designed around (in no apparent order). They are not rules, but provide a guide to important 'moving' features.

- Fixtures are patched to outputs with 'personalities' that map the controls of each specific fixture to the controls of the console, and automatically create colour groups and focus positions that can be used to quickly improvise a show.
- Lights can be positioned to certain acting areas and stored as focus presets that are used as references to that acting area during programming. If the acting area is moved, only the focus preset needs to be updated.
- Combinations of moving parameters can be stored into 'palettes' thereby setting, for example, 'all units centre stage with star gobo and rotating colours' which can be recalled from a single button.
- All moving light parameters are controlled as latest takes precedence, while dimmer intensities are treated as highest takes precedence. Masking is used to define which parameters are controlled from a playback at the moment.
- Plenty of control handles for fixture parameters (trackball, wheels).
- Plenty of submaster playback faders, which are the main controls.
- Each playback fader can run memories, cues or effects.
- Extensive effects with functions for improvising to musical beats per second.
- Usually a monitor support or displays to show parameters of fixtures.

Figure 2.16 Moving lights console with support for conventional lights (Sabre, courtesy Compulite)

Figure 2.17 Moving lights console with support for conventional lights (Wholehog II, courtesy Flying Pig Systems)

Figure 2.18 Moving lights console with support for conventional lights (Status Cue, courtesy High End)

- Multiple DMX outputs to support different lines of moving lights and dimmers.
- Often a support for conventional lights.
- Desks can often be linked, and have inputs for integration with other control systems.
- Accessories specifically for plotting moving lights such as, for example, a digitizer.

3 What does a lighting console consist of?

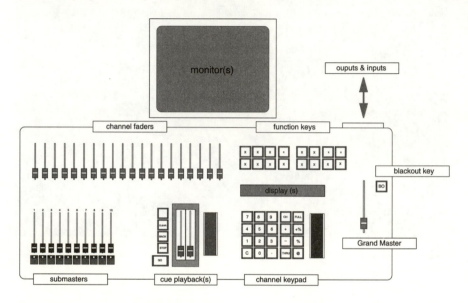

Figure 3.1 Example of a lighting console

All modern consoles share a few basic features, both on the inside and the outside. This is an introduction to these features, with a guide to chapters providing more information.

Hardware and software

A memory console has a hardware 'platform' and software running on that platform. Sometimes the platform is proprietary and sometimes it is a standard PC. Aspects of this are described in Chapter 1, 'Computers and lighting controls', p. 19.

Channels

The most basic component of a console is a channel. A channel is basically a control handle for setting intensities to dimmers which can be represented as a slider fader or a 'theatre style' channel keypad. Some consoles provide a combination of both (see Chapter 6). Channels and levels are plotted from these controls into lighting 'looks' that are stored into memories which can be played back from different 'electronic scenes' such as submasters or cue playbacks. These playbacks are sometimes called 'playback registers', 'stores' or 'control layers'. Since memories involving the same channels can be played back from several playbacks, there have to be certain rules for which level should be the output for a channel. There are two main rules for this, called highest takes precedence or latest takes precedence (see Chapter 4).

If a console supports scrollers and moving lights, the parameters of these are usually mapped as attributes to intensity channels (see Chapters 13 and 14).

Soft patch

The patch inside a console is called a soft patch, and is used to map the console channels to the outputs of the console which are sent to receiving lighting devices such as dimmers, moving lights and scrollers. Some consoles have to be patched before they can be used at all (see Chapter 5).

Submasters

Submasters are faders controlling the electronic equivalent of presetting scenes in a manual multi-scene console. Submasters allow many different lighting looks to be operated simultaneously at random choice, usually adding, or 'piling' intensities of memories to the output of the console on a highest takes precedence basis (see Chapter 7). Live consoles feature submasters as main playbacks while theatre consoles usually have them as a complement to the cue playbacks (see Chapter 2).

Cue playbacks

Cue playbacks are a combination of functions for playing back transitions between previously stored combinations of memories and fade times called cues. A cue playback usually has function keys for starting, stopping and resuming fades, sliders for taking manual control of a fader and some kind of 'incremental encoder' that can be used to control the rate of ongoing fades. This can be a wheel, a touchpad, a joystick, a trackball or something else.

Grand Master

Most consoles are equipped with a Grand Master, which is a control that can fade all channels in the system to a complete blackout without changing the individual settings in different playbacks. Therefore this control has to be set to full before any light can be output from the console at all. In systems controlling moving lights and scrollers the Grand Master will not usually affect these, allowing lights to be faded out without changing moving parameters.

Blackout key

Like the Grand Master, a blackout button will set all output levels to zero without altering the settings of the individual channels in the console. As with the Grand Master, this means that if this control is activated no light will be output from the console. A blackout key may be labelled BO or DBO, as in dead blackout.

Figure 3.2 Example of monitors and on-board displays (Courtesy ETC)

Function keys

A console will have a certain amount of function keys that give access to the programming features of the console. The quickest way to access a function is through a direct key, but many modern consoles have so many functions that a key to every one would simply make the console enormous. Many systems solve this partly with 'soft keys', which are function keys that will operate different functions in different modes (like the F keys on a personal computer). Some consoles provide touch screens for different soft keys.

Visual feedback – monitors and displays

A console has to provide visual feedback of some sort to the operator. In a manual console with channel faders the controls provide this feedback in a natural way, but in a memory console with a lot of the action going on 'under the hardware' either on-board displays or monitors are required to provide this kind of feedback. Many 'live' consoles can be operated without monitors (or optional) while most theatre consoles require a monitor to run the system. The advantage of a monitor is that information can be colour coded and displayed in different layouts.

Outputs and inputs

A console may have a number of different outputs and inputs to allow interaction with other devices and to support external accessories such as mouse or text keyboard. Here are some examples.

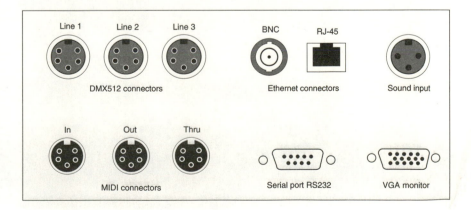

Figure 3.3 Lighting console connector examples

- video output to monitors
- keyboard input
- mouse/trackball input
- digitizer input (see Chapter 14)
- Ethernet (see Chapter 17)
- MIDI connectors (see Chapter 18)
- SMPTE time code connector (see Chapter 18)
- floppy drive (see Chapters 10 and 19)
- serial port connector, i.e. RS232 or 485 (see *Part 4 Communication*)
- output to dimmers, moving lights and scrollers (see *Parts 3 and 4*)
- DMX512 input (see Chapter 16)
- analogue out to dimmers or external equipment (see Chapter 16)
- analogue input for trigging console functions (see Chapter 10)
- input for remote focusing units
- support for a printer (see Chapter 11).

4 How do functions interact in a console?

A memory console consists of a number of 'electronic scenes' in the form of submasters and cue playbacks in which channel levels can be addressed and output to dimmers by manual controls such as submaster faders or cue playback controls. This chapter explains different ways in which these different playback functions may interact when the same channel level is addressed from several controls.

Highest takes precedence (HTP)

A dimmer (light) is controlled from 0 to 100%, but it can only physically have one intensity at any time, until it is set to a new one. In a manual single-scene desk with only one control 'handle' (channel fader) for each dimmer, it is pretty obvious where that intensity is output from. As soon as a console has more than one scene with a 'handle' for each channel, as in a manual two-scene presetting console, the highest level in any scene will be the one that is output to the dimmer controlling the light. This is called highest takes precedence or 'pile-on' behaviour.

If a channel follows this principle in a memory console with several playback controls such as submasters and cue playbacks, it means that it will always be set to the HTP sum of all controls that address it.

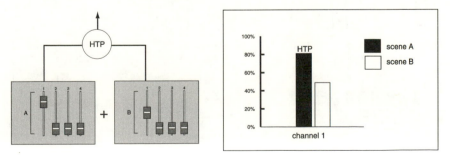

Figure 4.1 Highest takes precedence

HTP in submasters and cue playbacks

Submasters in memory consoles 'overlap', which means they can address the same channel outputs on this highest takes precedence basis. This means that a channel could be addressed from, for example, ten submasters at the same time. This channel can be brought to a higher level from any sub-master or channel control, but it can't be brought to a lower intensity unless it is faded down in every single submaster.

A cue playback usually consists of two 'electronic scenes', a 'live' scene which outputs the last cue and a 'next' scene from which a new cue will be faded into the live scene. The result of a transition between these cues is added on a highest takes precedence basis to the output of the submasters. When a console has more than one cue playback, and they interact on an HTP basis, the HTP sum of each cue playback will interact with all the other playbacks and submasters on an HTP basis.

There are different methods for bringing HTP channels down. One is an inhibitive submaster which can limit the output of any channel(s) regardless

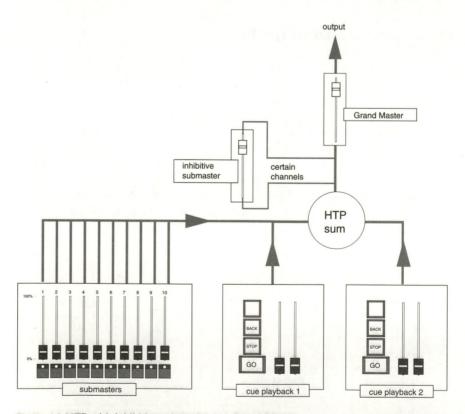

Figure 4.2 HTP with inhibitive submaster and Grand Master

of where they are output from, or a Grand Master that can limit the output of all channels (Figure 4.2).

Latest takes precedence (LTP)

In a manual single-scene desk, a channel fader can only be at one physical position (level) at any time, which means that the last level it was set to is the one it will be at. For example, if you set that channel fader to 50% it will remain there even if you are setting levels for other channels afterwards. When you decide to move it to (for example) 35%, that is where you will find it later because that was the last action performed with that channel fader. This is called latest takes precedence or the last action principle.

If a channel follows this principle in a memory console with several play-back controls such as submasters and cue playbacks, it means that it will always be set to the level of the control that last addressed it.

LTP in cue playbacks

In a memory console dimmer, intensities are usually treated as HTP chan-nels in all submasters but cue playbacks may treat channels as LTP either within the playback or between the playbacks for different reasons. A cue

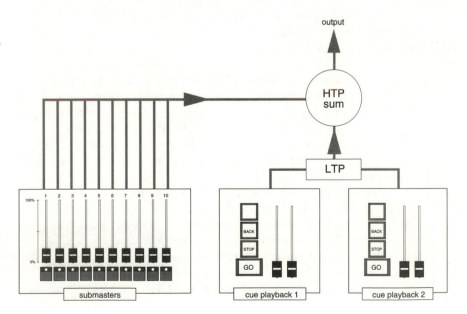

Figure 4.3 LTP cue playbacks

playback that operates on an LTP basis can make transitions between groups of channels in much the same way that channel faders can be moved independently by hand in a manual channel scene. If several cue playbacks operate on an LTP basis they are like 'several operators moving channels to new levels in the same channel scene', and each channel will be where 'somebody' last set it. This is the principle used in group fading and tracking cue playbacks (see Chapter 8). The result of LTP playbacks will still be HTPed with submasters before it is output (Figure 4.3).

LTP attributes

Channels that control parameters in moving lights or scrollers (attributes) are usually LTP in both submasters and cue playbacks. A channel that 'LTPs' like this in a console can only be under the control of one playback register at a time, until it is 'stolen' or 'passed on' to another playback. The advantage of this is that it is simple to gain control of that channel at any point simply by addressing it, since it will be 'stolen' from wherever it was controlled last, which is good for moving light functions, because when you want a fixture to move to a new position it is irrelevant where it was addressed from previously. Moving light attributes are usually not affected by the Grand Master fader or blackout function of a console, since this would mean that all moving lights and scrollers would rush to a zero position when these controls were used to dim light intensities.

One aspect of dealing with LTP attributes is deciding 'when' the control should be passed from one playback to another. There are a few solutions to this (varying from console to console).

1. As soon as a control is moved, LTP channels will be stolen to that control. This can be acceptable behaviour for cues, because usually a cue is intended to bring the actions on stage to a predefined setting and should be able to 'grab' attributes from all other playbacks. It is less practical as a general rule for submasters because they may also control intensities, and it won't be possible to move a submaster without 'grabbing' all attributes too.
2. As soon as a submaster is moved under a specified level (10%, for example), LTP channels will jump to the control of that submaster. This behaviour allows you to decide when you want a submaster to gain control of the LTP channels it controls. The only disadvantage is that if HTP dimmer intensities are controlled from the same submaster, the intensities have to be brought down to take control of LTP channels.
3. When a key for a specific playback is pressed, LTP channels will jump to that control. This way LTP channels can be transferred from one playback to another without changing dimmer intensities.

Masking

Another method for defining which LTP parameters should be affected by a new command is 'masking', which is often used for moving light parameters (see Chapter 14). In Figure 4.4 the colour parameter is masked from master 1 and all other parameters from master 2. Thanks to the masking there will be no control conflict between the masters if they are controlling the same moving fixture.

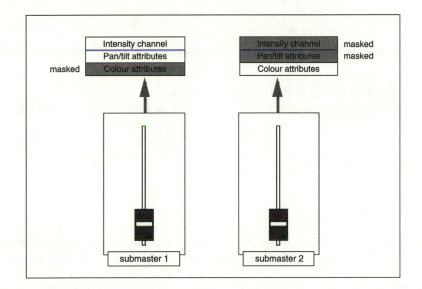

Figure 4.4 Masking

Channel control

There is usually a 'channel control' function in memory consoles that will either make changes directly in each playback register, or override all playbacks and capture control of any channel at any time, regardless of whether it is behaving as HTP or LTP. After such a modification has been made, the channel is intentionally 'released' back to the control of the submasters and cue playbacks in different ways depending on each console (Figure 4.5).

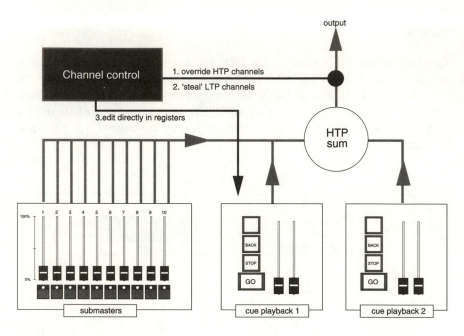

Figure 4.5 Channel control

Summary

- An HTP channel will be output at the highest level it is set to in any playback, and an LTP channel will be output at the last level assigned to it.
- Many consoles mix HTP and LTP behaviour. HTP is normally used for dimmer intensities in submasters and LTP for scroller and moving light attributes. Some consoles use LTP behaviour for dimmer intensities in cue playbacks, but the output from the playback will still be HTP with the submasters.

Part 2 – General Console Features

Introduction

Most consoles come with a thick manual explaining different control features from their 'own' point of view, and sometimes with a very individual terminology. The general features of all lighting consoles are similar, whatever they are called. The following chapters explain basic concepts such as *patching*, *channel control*, *macros*, *effects*, *submasters* and *cue playbacks* in a general way that can be applied to any console.

5 Patching

A patch in a lighting console is a 'software switchboard' that configures the way the console's control channels are mapped to the console's output channels. Originally a patch was a hardware switchboard between the outputs of a dimmer and the light loads, and this kind of patch is still used in some situations. This chapter describes both kinds of patches. To understand the terminology in this chapter, when it refers to the output signal of a console as 'analogue' or 'DMX512', it may help to read Chapter 16 first.

Load patching

A load patch is used when there are fewer dimmers than lights. This was common when dimmer technology was expensive and control systems were manual, which meant they couldn't handle many channels. Sometimes several hundred lights could be controlled by around 50 dimmer channels by using a load patch.

Nowadays dimmer technology is much more affordable and usually there is a dimmer per load in a lighting situation. In a fixed installation with one dimmer per load there is basically no need for a load patch. In touring dimmers there are still load patches though, since power multi-cables are often used from the dimmer outputs to the lights, and the light loads need to be evenly distributed among the dimmer outputs (Figure 5.1).

Control patching

A control patch is used to map the outputs of the console to the control side of the dimmers. When the output of a console is analogue it will arrive at the dimmers in a multi-connector that will map channel 1 to dimmer 1, channel 2 to dimmer 2 (etc.). Some dimmers have a small control patch so that a different configuration can be made, which is like a small telephone switchboard in the dimmer. When the output of a console is a multiplexed signal like DMX512, the control patch can be moved into the realm of the console, where it is called a soft patch.

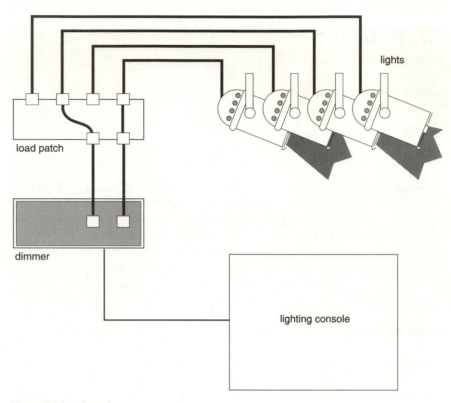

Figure 5.1 Load patch

Soft and proportional patching

A soft patch will map the control channels of a console to its multiplexed outputs, which are 512 in each DMX line. For example, a console may have only 24 channels and one DMX line, which makes it possible to address 512 dimmers by mapping several dimmers to each control channel. Many consoles can scale the output of each multiplexed output, which is called a proportional soft patch.

Some consoles require the patch to be set up before a new show can be started and some have a default patch where channel 1 is mapped to output 1, channel 2 to output 2 (etc.). In either case a soft patch can be used for different things (Figures 5.2 and 5.3).

(a) *More dimmers than console channels*
A soft patch will allow a few control channels to address several dimmers. In concert lighting hundreds of lights can be patched to a small and 'playable' console. If certain lights should operate at a generally lower intensity than

```
8:13PM   5/26/06        MUX ORDERED PATCH 1    No Title         GM=FL/FL
                                                                  Status
MUX    1     2     3     4     5     6     7     8     Intensity
CHN    1     2     3     4     5     6     7     8     Total  350
      100%  100%  100%  100%  100%  100%  100%  100%  InUse  350
MUX    9    10    11    12    13    14    15    16     Free     0
CHN    9    10    11    12    13    14    15    16
      100%  100%  100%  100%  100%  100%  100%  100%  Attribute
                                                      Total  250
MUX   17    18    19    20    21    22    23    24     InUse    0
CHN   17    18    19    20    21    22    23    24     Free   250
      100%  100%  100%  100%  100%  100%  100%  100%
MUX   25    26    27    28    29    30    31    32     Live     1
CHN   25    26    27    28    29    30    31    32     Edit     1
      100%  100%  100%  100%  100%  100%  100%  100%    Wheel
MUX   33    34    35    36    37    38    39    40
CHN   33    34    35    36    37    38    39    40
      100%  100%  100%  100%  100%  100%  100%  100%
MUX   41    42    43    44    45    46    47    48
CHN   41    42    43    44    45    46    47    48
      100%  100%  100%  100%  100%  100%  100%  100%
MUX   49    50    51    52    53    54    55    56
CHN   49    50    51    52    53    54    55    56     v1.4
      100%  100%  100%  100%  100%  100%  100%  100%

MUX ORDERED PATCH 1:
Set patch for Level, Colour, and Non-Dim 2SHUT  8MACRO 9MACRO 1MACRO 1Append1SAVE
channels                          |DOWN! |  982 |  983 0  984 1FxStep2SHOW
```

Figure 5.2 Screen proportional soft patch (Courtesy Strand Lighting)

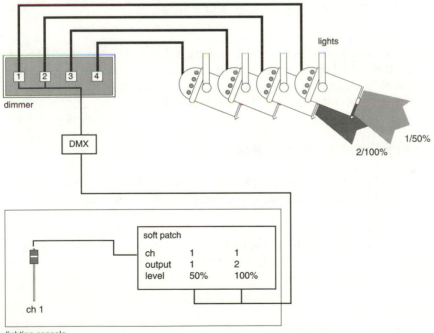

Figure 5.3 Proportional soft patch

the others, they can be patched proportionally (see Figure 5.3). The individual dimmers patched to the same control channel will always operate at the same time, which has to be taken into account from a design point of view from the very start.

(b) *Organizing channel numbers*
In theatre lighting and other situations where many dimmers are controlled from systems with many control channels, the soft patch is rarely used to group several dimmers to a single control channel. Instead it is used so that console channels correspond to lights are numbered in the rig. For example, all backlights can be patched to console channels 1–20, all sidelights to console channels 21–40, specials to 41–50, etc. This kind of logical numbering makes it easy to find individual lights in a large rig.

(c) *Extending lamp hours*
If an output is set to operate at 95%, it means those lights will never operate at 100%, which will extend the lifespan of those light bulbs (almost double). Proportional scaling can also be used to match light sources of different intensities, for example a 500 W light used together with a 650 W light.

WARNING: Avoid using a 230 V dimmer proportionally set to 50% for 120V equipment, because the transients will still be 230 V, see Chapter 12.

(d) *Continuous output*
Some patches have a 'hot patching' function that sets an output channel to be at 100% at all times, which is useful if a dimmer is used to power a non-dimmable instrument like a smoke machine, for example. This may also be the function of a dimmer response curve, see Chapter 12.

Channel numbering confusion

With load patches, control patches and multiple DMX lines there are many different factors that can cause numbering confusion in a rig.

(a) *Console channels*
The channels that can be individually controlled from a console are called console channels. For example, in a 120-channel console these channels are usually numbered 1–120.

(b) *DMX channels*
The amount of dimmers or other lighting devices that can be addressed from a console depends on how many DMX channels the console can output. One DMX line can control up to 512 outputs, and there may be several.

DMX output channels are always 1–512 in each DMX line. This can get confusing when there is more than one DMX output, because there will be a DMX channel 1 in line 1 and a DMX channel 1 in line 2. Most consoles 'hide' this by displaying the outputs of the second DMX line as 513–1024.

(c) *Lighting devices' DMX address*
Each lighting device that is responding to DMX channels has an address that defines which DMX channels it should respond to. This means that a dimmer set to DMX address 1 that is controlled by DMX line 2 could be mapped to control channel 513 in the console.

(d) *Load patches and circuits*
A dimmer may be routed through a load patch to a multi-cable feeding a circuit to which a light can be connected. This circuit may have a number of its own, for example 'Circuit 23 in rig section 4 = 234'.

(e) *Unit numbers*
Since a dimmer may have more than one light connected to it, there can be an identification number for each lighting unit too.

Basically a rig with one light to each circuit, one circuit to each dimmer, one dimmer to each console channel, fewer than 512 channels and no load or control patching will provide no numbering confusion. This is not unusual in smaller systems controlling only conventional lights, but as soon as a soft patch and some moving lights are added there is good reason to have a thorough documentation of the channel assignments.

6 Channels

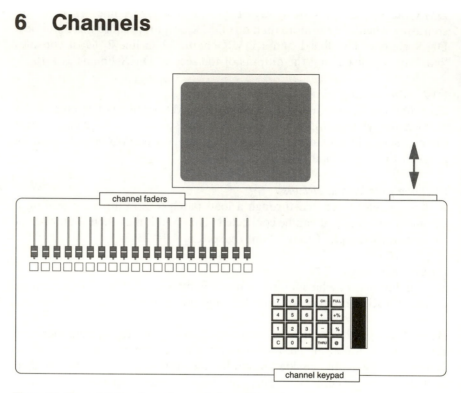

Figure 6.1 Channel faders, bump keys and channel keypad

Channels are the most basic component of a lighting console, they are the individual control 'handles' that are used to set dimmer intensities 0–100%. A lighting console is primarily designed for accessing channels and playing them back in different ways, either manually with faders and bump buttons or by fading between whole memories with individual channels and levels stored in advance (using submasters and cue playbacks). There is a special function for recalling frequently used combinations of channels called Groups which is common in theatre consoles and is described at the end of this chapter.

General

A console can address channels in different ways. The most basic solution is physical faders and bump buttons because they provide quick and direct access to individual channels. This is why 'live' consoles and smaller manual consoles usually have these (see Chapter 2). In a memory console individual channels don't have to be physical faders, they can be 'electronic handles' which are accessed from a 'theatre style' channel control keypad and specific functions for controlling channels (in calculator style). A channel keypad allows whole list of channels to be selected individually or as groups, which means hundreds of channels can be addressed in the same way. This chapter will mainly be about aspects of channel keypad control since channel faders were explained in Chapter 2.

One channel does not necessarily equal a single light source. One channel can be patched to several dimmers (see Chapter 5), and one or more lights can be controlled from the same dimmer (see Fig. 6.2).

'Theatre style' channel keypad

The most common method of addressing channels in theatre consoles and consoles with many channels is a numerical keypad and channel/level-setting functions. An advantage of keypad control is that whole lists of

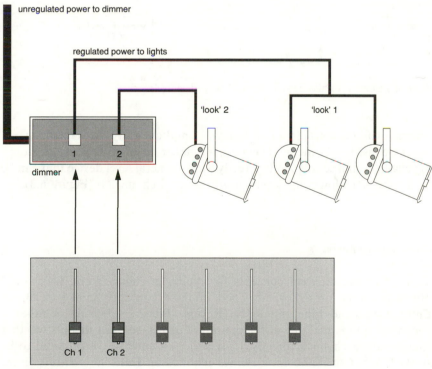

Figure 6.2 Channels controlling lights

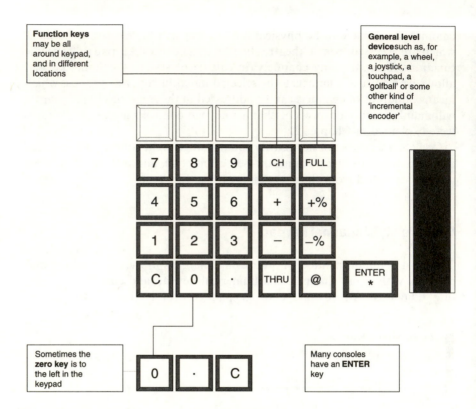

Figure 6.3 Example of 'theatre style' channel keypad controls

channels can be selected and set to levels simultaneously. A channel keypad usually consists of a numeric keypad, a number of function keys for grouping channels and setting levels directly plus a general level device that can be used to raise or lower the levels of any selected channel(s) (Figure 6.3).

Command syntaxes

There are three different concepts for typing in channels and levels (and other functions) on a keypad. Each of these concepts known as Direct Entry, Command Line and RPN (Reverse Polish Notation), is called a command syntax and one of the main differences between them is whether changes affect channels directly, or whether an enter key is required to be stroked first. Command Line always requires an Enter key, Direct Entry requires it in certain situations and RPN never requires an Enter key. Direct Entry and Command Line are language oriented (English) allowing a lighting designer to 'speak' commands more or less the way they are entered by the console operator (unless these two are the same person).

Direct Entry

One of the first command syntaxes implemented in a memory console was Direct Entry (sometimes called At mode). The syntax is based on simulating the English language 'as spoken' and requires no separate Enter key to complete channel and level commands, but an Enter key is used for other functions of the console.

There are two main objectives behind the evolution of this syntax and the different dialects:

(a) To simulate commands 'as spoken' (to simplify learning).
(b) To have few keystrokes to finish a command (to save time).

• *Selecting a combination of channels*
With Direct Entry any number entered on the keypad is automatically treated as a channel unless a prefix key has been used to make the keypad treat it as, for example, a cue, submaster or group. The functions used to select a combination of channels are AND, EXCEPT, THRU (to select a range of channels) and ALL. With these functions the verbal command 'select channels 1 and 5 through 10, except channel 7' can be done with the command syntax '1_AND_5_THRU_10_EXCEPT_7'.

Since this English 'grammar' doesn't make sense in all languages, many consoles replace these functions with symbols that don't need translation.

AND is replaced by +
EXCEPT is replaced by −
THRU is replaced by < – >
ALL: all channels are usually selected by pressing ENTER. ENTER can also be a symbol in some systems; it is represented by [*] in Strand systems, for example.

Examples
1. The verbal command 'select channels 1 and 4' translates to the key syntax: '1 + 4'.
2. The verbal command 'select channels 1 and 5 through 10, except channel 7' translates to the key syntax '1 + 5 THRU 10 − 7'.

• *Setting levels*
There are different 'dialects' of Direct Entry when it comes to setting levels. After a combination of channels has been selected an 'AT' key is used to

announce that the next numbers entered on the keypad will be a level for those channels. Because no Enter key is used for setting levels, the console will act as soon as 'enough' data has been input. One dialect treats every number as a level, for example a level of 45 will first be 4% and then 45%. Another dialect treats all levels as multiples of ten which means that entering, for example, 4 will give 40%, but it also means that a level of 4% or 44% has to be entered in a different way. These are the three most common dialects for setting levels.

Level	1 Digit Direct	2 Digit Direct	2 + 1 Direct mode
1–9%	0.1–0.9	01–09	1–9
10–90	1–9	10–90	10–90 (OR 1–9 + ENTER)
11–99	1.1–9.9	11–99	11–99
100%	FULL key	FULL key	FULL key

1 Digit Direct multiplies each level by ten, saving one key (0) when entering a level of 10–90%. In return one more key (the decimal point) is required for any other kind of level.

2 Digit Direct uses normal level values except for levels 0–9% of which require a preceding 0 so that the console can 'know' that the command is terminated.

2 + 1 Direct combines both methods in a third dialect where all levels can be entered normally. If one digit is entered it is treated as a level of 0–9% and if a second digit is entered both are treated as a whole, which means that, for example, a level of 45 will first be 4% and then 45%. Some consoles also provide the option of pressing Enter after one digit which will multiply that by ten, as in 1 Digit Direct.

All three dialects use a [FULL] key to avoid entering three keys [1] [0] [0] to set a level of 100%. Systems that don't have a [FULL] key provide this function by double pressing the AT key, which is sometimes represented by the symbol '@'.

Command Line

The Command Line syntax is the most 'computer-oriented' syntax because it requires an Enter key to be stroked before any command will affect the functions of the console. One advantage of this is that complex and long commands can be 'stacked', revised and executed simultaneously.

It is similar to Direct Entry in being 'language-oriented', allowing whole 'sentences' in English to be entered more or less 'as spoken'.

Setting channel 1 at 50% is translated to: [1] [@] [5] [0] [*]

1   @   50   * (ENTER)
The command line   The execute key

To make the syntax even clearer the system command line display will 'fill in' the 'missing words' (underlined in the example) of a command, so in fact the command above will be displayed on the command line as:

Channel 1 @ 50 *

Channels are selected with the same functions as Direct Entry, and levels are typed normally. Command Line is consistent also for other functions, extending the 'grammar' to a variety of situations. For example, when a lighting state has been set up and is recorded in a cue, it allows fade times to be set in the same 'line':

RECORD in CUE 1 TIME 4 *

Split fade or delay (wait) times are among the few functions not entered in a logical 'grammar', instead a '/' is used to divide up-times from down-times. Recording Cue 1 with an up-time of 3 s and a down time of 5 s translates like this:

RECORD in CUE 1 TIME 3 / 5 *

The same command with a delay down-time of 6 s translates like this:

RECORD in CUE 1 TIME 3 / 5 DELAY / 6 *

Another example showing the possible complexity of a single command line is the following, where cues 1 through 10 are modified simultaneously to a split time of 4 s up 6 s down, a delay up of 3 s and a wait time of 2 s:

CUE 1 THRU 10 TIME 4 / 6 DELAY 3 WAIT 2 *

NOTE: Command Line originated in the United States in the Light Palette (Strand, 1980) and is a commonly preferred syntax in consoles used for Broadway productions and other large venues where lighting designers and operators are used to it. The 'original' syntax of the Light Palette has been refined in different products over the years and may differ slightly from system to system.

Reverse Polish Notation (RPN)

This syntax is designed to produce immediate display updates and it can be applied to any function in a system without requiring an Enter key. RPN is not language oriented like Direct Entry or Command Line, instead it is based on all entries to be made with a simple 'grammar' of two 'words'. The first word is a number and the second is a function. The reason it is called 'reverse' is that most other syntaxes are entered 'function-number'.
　　Setting channel 1 @ 50% translates into: 1 CH 50 @

1	CH	50	@
number	function	number(s)	function

With RPN all functions start with a number entry, which means there are no 'modes' or prefix keys telling the keypad to receive entries as channels, cues, submasters, times or groups. Instead, you could say that all function keys are suffix keys with a 'built-in' Enter function. This command structure allows several functions to be stacked after each other, being executed and displayed as they are entered.

Example
Select channels 5 through 10 at 50% and store as cue 4 with a time of 6 s translates into:

5_CH_10_THRU_50_@_4_RECORD_6_TIME

Since every second key is a function key the system will be able to display what is going on all the time, for example 5 CH 10 THRU will show channels 5–10 selected on the displays, while most Direct Entry dialects won't display those channels until the @ key has been pressed.

Combinations of channels are selected with the same functions as in Direct Entry ('+', '−', 'THRU' and 'ALL') and levels are entered normally (except that the level key is pressed after they are entered). The keypad never assumes automatically that a number is a channel, which means that a CH key is always used after entering a channel number.

NOTE: RPN is mostly used in AVAB consoles, and usually Direct Entry can be selected as an option.

Summary of command syntaxes

Which syntax is 'better' than another is probably a question of what an operator is used to working with.

- Direct Entry is entered 'as spoken' in English and provides short command chains for selecting channels and setting levels. There are dialects for how levels are entered and an Enter key is required for some functions.
- Command Line will not act on a command until an Enter key is stroked and is entered 'as spoken' in English. Long and complex commands can be stacked and executed with a single key (Enter) after being revised on the Command Line Display of the console.
- RPN enters all functions as 'number-function' which means all commands are acted on and displayed as they are entered. No Enter key is required.

Here are some examples of how the syntaxes are applied in different situations.

Select channel 1 (live) to general level device (wheel, for example):

1 Digit direct	[1]	[Wheel]
2 Digit direct	[1]	[Wheel]
2 + 1 Digit direct	[1]	[Wheel]
Command line	[1]	[*] [Wheel]
RPN	[1]	[Wheel]

Set channel 1 to 5%:

1 Digit direct	[1]	[@]	[0]	[.]	[5]
2 Digit direct	[1]	[@]	[0]	[5]
2 + 1 Digit direct	[1]	[@]	[5]	
Command line	[1]	[@]	[5]	[*]
RPN	[1]	[CH]	[5]	[@]

Set channel 1 to 50%:

1 Digit direct	[1]	[@]	[5]	
2 Digit direct	[1]	[@]	[5]	[0]
2 + 1 Digit direct	[1]	[@]	[5]	[0]
Command line	[1]	[@]	[5]	[0]	[*]
RPN	[1]	[CH]	[5]	[0]	[@]

Set channel 1 at 63%:

1 Digit direct	[1]	[@]	[6]	[.]	[3]
2 Digit direct	[1]	[@]	[6]	[3]	
2 + 1 Digit direct	[1]	[@]	[6]	[3]	
Command line	[1]	[@]	[6]	[3]	[*]
RPN	[1]	[CH]	[6]	[3]	[@]

Set channels 1 + 5 at 100%:

1 Digit direct	[1]	[+]	[5]	[FULL]	
2 Digit direct	[1]	[+]	[5]	[FULL]	
2 + 1 Digit direct	[1]	[+]	[5]	[FULL]	
Command line	[1]	[+]	[5]	[FULL]	
RPN	[1]	[CH]	[5]	[+] [@]	[@]

Store current settings as cue 1:

1 Digit direct	[Cue]	[1]	[Record]	
2 Digit direct	[Cue]	[1]	[Record]	
2 + 1 Digit direct	[Cue]	[1]	[Record]	
Command line	[Record Cue]		[1]	[*]
RPN	[1]	[Record]		

Fade to cue 3 using programmed times:

1 Digit direct	[Goto]	[3]	[*]
2 Digit direct	[Goto]	[3]	[*]
2 + 1 Digit direct	[Goto]	[3]	[*]
Command line	[Goto]	[3]	[*]
RPN	[3]	[Goto]	

Groups

Frequently used combinations of channels and levels can in some systems be recorded into units called groups. These groups can then be added together to create new looks which speed up programming when many channels are involved.

For example, if channels 1–8 are backlights they can be balanced into a look with the following intensities:

Channel	1	2	3	4	5	6	7	8
Level	80%	60%	60%	55%	55%	60%	60%	80%

By storing this as a group it can be recalled and added or subtracted pro-portionally with a single command instead of by selecting the channels one by one.

(a) *Reselecting the same group settings*
Channels 1–8 can be set to those intensities by recalling that group at 100%.

(b) *Adding the group proportionally*
Channels 1–8 can also be set to a proportional level of the stored levels in the group, for example GROUP 1 @ 50% would give the following result:

Channel	1	2	3	4	5	6	7	8
Level	40%	30%	30%	27%	27%	30%	30%	40%

(c) *Selecting the channels for modification*
A group can be a quick way to select channels for modification with a general fading device like a wheel.

(d) *Adding and subtracting groups*
Groups can be added and subtracted as a short-cut to selecting certain channels.

For example, in a design with two six-bars with PAR64 lights as back-lights, with three colours alternating amber, green and blue, the following four groups could be stored to simplify plotting looks:

Two six-bars with filters.

Group 1: All amber	< Ch 1,4,7,10 >
Group 2: All green	< Ch 2,5,8,11 >
Group 3: All blue	< Ch 3,6,9,12 >
Group 4: Backlights	< Ch 1–12 >

All blue and green backlights can be selected in two ways: group 2 + group 3 OR group 4 − group 1. Both methods are faster than identifying and selecting the channels one by one.

7 Submasters

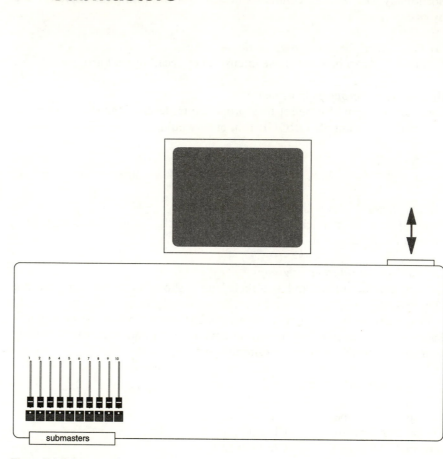

Figure 7.1 Submasters in a console

In a manual desk a submaster is a general fader for a complete channel scene in which a lighting look can be preset and faded up or down by the submaster fader. In a memory console a submaster is a general fader for an 'electronic channel scene' where channel levels in the form of memories or effects can be controlled and faded with the submaster fader. Most memory consoles have submasters for playing back lighting looks as a main or side component of a performance. This chapter is about the general features of submasters.

In 'live' consoles submasters are the main playbacks, and shows are set up to be played back by fading from one submaster to another with the possibility of adding (piling) several memories simultaneously and using the bump keys to flash complete lighting looks. This is a practical and common method in 'one-off' situations with little preplanning. In theatre consoles submasters are often used to speed up programming by mixing combinations of frequently-used channels, or for 'specials' like follow spots.

Additive or inhibitive

There are two ways in which a submaster can affect intensities from the other submasters and cue playbacks.

(a) *Additive mode*
An additive master will add intensities proportionally to the rest of the output in a 'pile-on', or highest takes precedence (HTP) manner. Submasters controlling latest takes precedence (LTP) attributes for moving lights or scrollers can interact in various ways (see Chapter 4).

(b) *Inhibitive mode*
An inhibitive submaster limits the intensities of certain channels from the output like a selective Grand Master. Basically it prevents channels assigned to it from exceeding the level of the inhibitive submaster fader (see Chapter 4). This can be used to create, for example, a separate 'Grand Master' for fading out all channels in front of the curtain in a theatre (called front of house channels) during curtain calls.

Submaster faders

In a modern console the physical control for a submaster is usually a slider fader, but it can be any mechanical solution that allows continuous control, like a thumb wheel or a trackpad. Some systems even provide virtual submasters, which means they exist in the software, but don't necessarily have physical controls and are accessed from function keys or a mouse.

Flashing a submaster – bump keys

Bump keys are momentary keys usually located next to a submaster. Pressing a bump key will affect how a submaster contributes intensities to the output in one of the following ways:

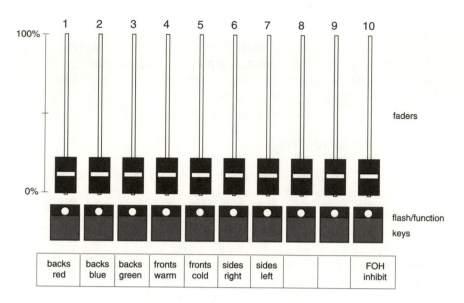

Figure 7.2 Example of submasters

- *Bump/add/flash*

In this mode, pressing the bump key usually brings the contents of the submaster on stage instantly, adding them to the outputs of the other play-backs. Normally the levels are maintained on stage until the key is released.

- *Solo/kill/swop*

In this mode the submaster content will be brought up, and all other sub-masters will be 'killed' until the bump button is released. This can be used to change the output on stage from the sum of all submasters to a specific scene and then back.

- *Latch/toggle*

In this mode one press will bring the submaster up, and a second press will bring it down. Some consoles can use fade times in a mode like this, making the bump key a GO button for that submaster. The simplest fade time for a submaster is a single fade time, but some consoles allow up-, wait- and down times for memories in each submaster.

Submaster pages

A submaster 'page' is a function for storing and recalling information to a whole block of submasters. In this way the same submaster faders can be used to control a number of different memories in a show. For example, if submasters 1–24 control memories 1–24 and more memories are required, a new page can be loaded to the same submasters containing memories 25–48 (replacing 1–24). If a submaster is active when a new page is selected, the information will usually be updated when that master is faded to zero, which makes it possible to change submaster pages without affecting the lights on stage.

8 Cue playbacks

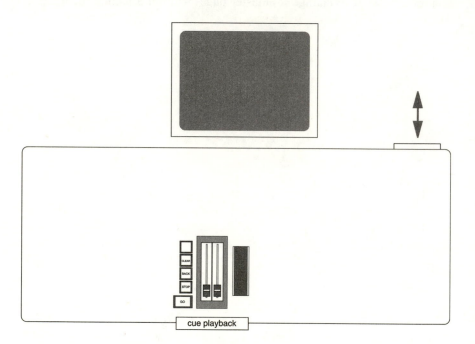

Figure 8.1 Cue playback in a console

The word cue may be used for many things. It can be the signal given by a stage manager, or dictated by the action on stage to carry out a previously plotted change of light, sound or scenery. Depending on the lighting design and console being used, this may involve several actions such as fading manually and bumping flash buttons, or just pressing a GO button. In a memory lighting console a cue is a stored combination of channel levels and fade times that are activated by that GO button. This chapter is about how cues are stored, edited and played back in the cue playbacks of different consoles.

What can a cue consist of?

A cue consists of channels and levels that are to be replayed, together with fade times for the transition from the previous cue, and information on how the cue should affect currently fading cues when it is started (if there are any). Each cue is stored with an identification number (whole or decimal) and sometimes a text to help the operator know when the cue is to be activated.

Example

Cue 5
Text: 'Start when John falls off stage'
Up-fading channels: 10 s
Down-fading channels: 4 s
Channels 5/50%, 3/40%, 23/100%

The transition from one cue to another can be initiated by a GO button or it can be done manually with slider faders. If the transition replaces all channel intensities of the previous cue it is called a crossfade, and if channels that have the same levels in both cues remain still during the fade it is a dipless crossfade (see 'The concept of manual desks', p. 35). If the transition moves only some channels to new levels without replacing the whole previous cue it is called a move fade.

The order in which cues can be stored

As cues are recorded they are usually stored in ascending numerical order in a cue list, or a sequence. In a 'one-off' situation with no rehearsal, cues can usually be 'played' in random order depending on what the action on stage dictates. In a sequential production that is going to run several nights, it is preferable to have the cues stored in the order they are to be played back so that the operator can concentrate fully on timing the fades. Therefore, most consoles provide functions for editing the cue list by inserting, deleting and copying cues, or making a link from one cue to another to create a loop or new playback order.

Editing the cue list

The order in which cues are recorded is not the order in which they appear in the cue list. They are usually sorted numerically, so recording cues 3, 5 and 1 will provide the following cue list:

Cue 1
Cue 3
Cue 5

Inserting cues

Inserting a cue between cue 1 and 3 is done by recording it as cue 2 and letting the automatic sorting take care of the insertion:

Cue 1
Cue 2
Cue 3
Cue 5

Inserting a cue between 1 and 2 is usually solved using decimal cues. For example, recording cue 1.5 will provide the following result:

Cue 1
Cue 1.5
Cue 2
Cue 3
Cue 5

This will work fine until you need to insert a cue between 1.5 and 1.6. There are different approaches to solving this:

(a)   Most consoles will solve this by recording the cue with a high number (99, for example) and making two links, playing back cue 99 after cue 1.5 and then playing back cue 1.6 after cue 99.

Cue 1
Cue 1.5   Link to cue 99
Cue 1.6
Cue 2
Cue 3
Cue 5
.

.

.

Cue 99   Link to cue 1.6

(b)   Few consoles support two-digit decimal cues, but if one does, this can be solved by recording cue 1.55:

Cue 1
Cue 1.5
Cue 1.55
Cue 1.6
Cue 2

(c)   Some consoles (Wholehog II and AVAB systems, for example) have a 'free sequence' that allows cues to be rearranged out of order, in this case any cue number can be inserted between the cues:

Cue 1
Cue 1.5
Cue 99
Cue 1.6
Cue 2

(d)   Some consoles (the ETC Expression line, for example) have solved this with subroutines where cues can be sorted in any order:

Cue 1
Cue 1.5
     Subroutine
          Cue 99
Cue 1.6
Cue 2

Deleting cues

In most systems the only way to remove a cue from the sequence is to delete it. If you don't want to lose the information in a cue you could copy it to the end of the cue list or create a link to bypass it.

Copying cues

Sometimes you may want to repeat a cue, or use the levels in a cue as a foundation for creating a new cue. Most systems can copy a cue by bringing it up on stage and recording it again with a new cue number, and some provide special functions for this.

Links

Many systems have a feature that will create a link from one cue to another during playback. This can be used to insert a cue between existing cues as described earlier, but it can also be used to play back cues completely out of sequence, to skip a series of cues or to create a loop of cues repeating automatically.

In this example a link is used to skip cues 3–6 during playback, without deleting them:

Cue 1
Cue 2   Link to cue 7
Cue 3
Cue 4
Cue 5
Cue 6
Cue 7

In this example a link from cue 4 to cue 2 is used to create an endless effect loop out of these three cues:

Cue 1
Cue 2
Cue 3
Cue 4   Link to cue 2

In this example a link is used to move cues 2–4 to after cue 7, for example due to a change in the play requiring this (the alternative would have been to copy cues 2–4 to 8–10 and delete the original 2–4):

Cue 1
Cue 1.5   Link to cue 5   < first link to cue 5
Cue 2
Cue 3
Cue 4   Link to cue 8   < third link down to cue 8
Cue 5
Cue 6
Cue 7   Link to cue 2   < second link back to cue 2
Cue 8
Cue 9
Cue 10

In a system with a 'free sequence', the same problem could be solved in this way:

Step	Cue
1	1
2	1.5
3	5
4	6
5	7
6	2
7	3
8	4
9	8
10	9
11	10

In a system with subroutines, the same problem could be solved in this way:

Cue 1.5
    Subroutine
        Cue 5
        Cue 6
        Cue 7
        Cue 2
        Cue 3
        Cue 4
Cue 8
Cue 9
Cue 10

Cue fade times

The fade times of a cue will affect the transition of channels fading to new levels when that cue is started. These levels can be either higher, lower or equal to the currently output levels. To make it possible to recreate a complex fade from a GO button, there is a variety of different fade times that can be stored with a single cue, but there is no standard definition of fade times. For example, a wait time can be three different things (see 'Summary of time terminologies', p. 97).

    Cues can have the following times:

- fade up/down
- delay up/down

- wait from GO to start next cue
- wait from completed fade to start next cue
- part times within a cue
- alert, operator warning between cues
- rate: a 'scaling' of all times in %.

Fade up/down times

The up-fade is the fade time for channels moving to a higher level when the cue is run, and the down-fade is the time for channels moving to a lower level. This is also called in/out times (see 'Summary of time terminologies', p. 97).

- *Single fade time*
The simplest fade is when up-going and down-going channels are faded on the same time. This is called a single fade time.

- *Split fade times*
In a split fade the up-going channels will fade on a different time to the down-going channels.

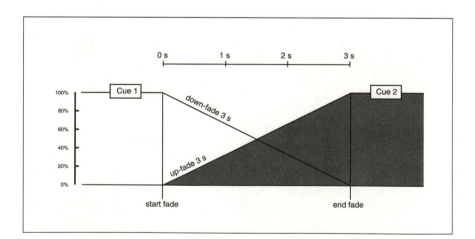

Figure 8.2 Single fade time

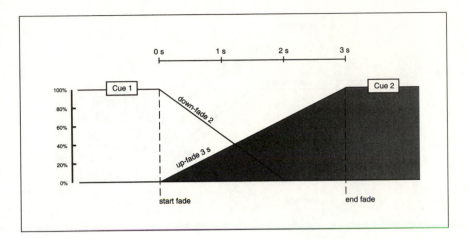

Figure 8.3 Split fade time

Delay up/down

A delay is a time that elapses between starting a cue, and when the actual fade begins. This is also called a wait time (see 'Summary of time terminologies', p. 97).

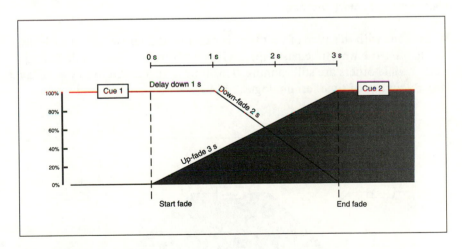

Figure 8.4 Single delay (down)

Split delay up/down

Some systems allow a separate delay of the up-fade and the down-fade. Applying this will result in no fade at all when the cue is executed, since

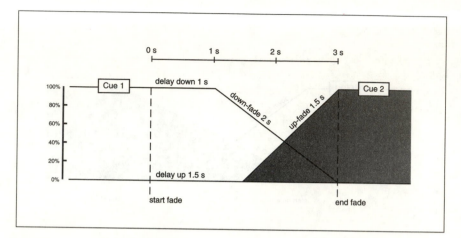

Figure 8.5 Split delay (up and down)

both fades are delayed. This can be useful for timing purposes, when the natural cueing point takes place before the fading is requested.

Wait from GO to start next cue

When a cue with this type of wait time is run, the next cue will automatically be run after the wait time has elapsed. This is useful when new fades can be started while others are still running. This time is also called follow or delay (see 'Summary of time terminologies', p. 97).

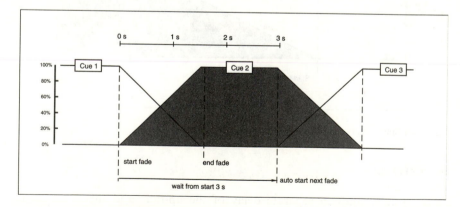

Figure 8.6 Wait from start of fade

Wait from completed fade to start next cue

This type of wait time starts elapsing after the previous cue has been completed. This is useful with crossfades, since a cue has to be completed before a new one is started, or it will change the timing of all channels in the previous cue. This time is also called hold, link, chain or loop (see 'Summary of time terminologies', p. 97).

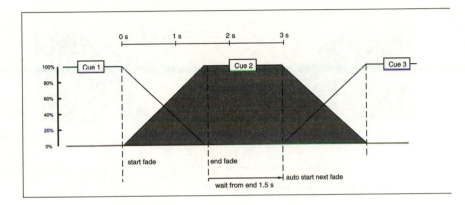

Figure 8.7 Wait from end of previous cue

Part times within a cue

Many systems allow a cue to have parts with separate fade and delay times in the same cue. In a crossfade, the parts will all have to be completed before a new cue can be started, but in a move fade or a fade in a tracking console, several parts can fade 'transparently', regardless of each other, provided the same channels are not involved. This is called parts, multipart cues, special times and time groups (see 'Summary of time terminologies', p. 97).

Example:

Cue 1
Cue 2
      Part 1
      Part 2
Cue 3
Cue 4

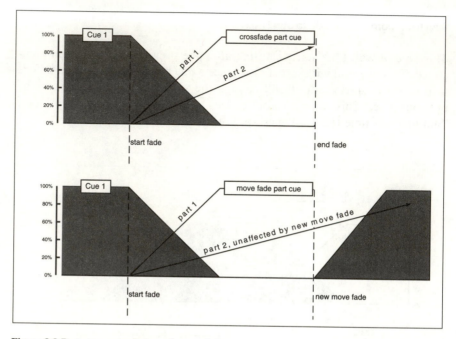

Figure 8.8 Part cues, crossfade and move fade

Alert, operator warning between cues

This time will alert the operator to the fact that 'usually' the next cue is run a certain elapsed time counting from the end of the previous fade. This is useful to help a console operator get into the rhythm of a new design. This is called alert or elapsed (see 'Summary of time terminologies', p. 97).

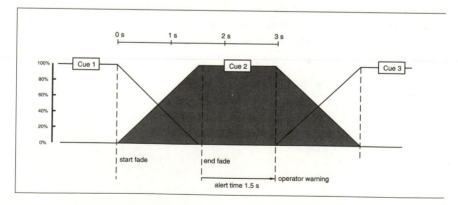
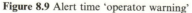

Figure 8.9 Alert time 'operator warning'

Rate

A cue with an up-fade of 4 s and a down fade of 2 s can be 'scaled' with a rate function in some consoles. A rate of, for example, 200% would extend the up-fade to 8 s and the down fade to 4 s. This is an extremely useful function for 'tweaking' fade times for a cue.

Summary of time terminologies

In those cases where the term used here for a time differs, it will probably be listed below. All consoles do not necessarily have all times and there may be more terms than those listed.

- *Fade up/down*
AVAB: in/out
Compulite: in/out

- *Delay up/down*
ADB: Wait
ETC: Wait
Transtechnik: Wait
Compulite: Wait

- *Wait from GO to start next cue*
AVAB: Follow
ETC: Follow
Transtechnik: Delay

- *Wait from completed fade to start next cue*
ADB: Link/Chain
Arri: Link
Transtechnik: Hold
Compulite: Loop

- *Part times within a cue*
ADB: Special times
AVAB: Time groups
ETC: Multipart cues
Strand: Part cues

- *Alert, operator warning between cues*
AVAB: Alert/Elapsed

What is a cue playback?

The individual cues are stored in a cue list, and the combination of faders and function keys that can be used to make transitions between cues are usually grouped together in a cue playback. Most cue playbacks share some general functions even though the implementation and terminology can vary between different consoles:

- faders for manual transitions, these may be slider faders or wheels
- a rate control for ongoing fades in the form of a wheel, slider, joystick 'golf ball' or touch pad
- a GO button that 'launches' the next cue
- a STOP function to 'halt' an ongoing fade
- a RESUME function to resume a fade halted with STOP
- a GO BACK function to fade to the previous cue
- a CUT function to load a new cue directly to the playback
- a CLEAR function to clear the playback
- a LOAD function that loads a cue to the playback.

In addition to these there may be other functions, like direct keys for stepping to the next or last (previous) cue in the cue list or jumping to a specific cue.

The design of a cue playback, and how cues are plotted, edited and played back, depends on the playback philosophy of the console. There are three main approaches: preset-oriented, group fading and tracking cue playbacks. The following sections describe general aspects of each that apply in most cases, but there may be consoles mixing features from more than one philosophy in attempts to satisfy different users.

Preset-oriented playbacks

Basically, the philosophy of a preset-oriented cue playback is that each new cue completely replaces the readings of the previous cue, similar to a manual two-scene desk, which crossfades between channel settings in two scenes (see 'The concept of manual desks', p. 35). Normally a playback consists of function keys and two faders, one addressing the 'live' cue and one addressing the 'next' cue, which means that cues can be 'loaded' and 'cleared' from each fader. The faders operate individual 'scenes' on an HTP basis, which means the readings of one fader can be 'piled' on top of the other during a manual fade, with the exception of channels not changing level which remain 'dipless'. Once the transition to a new cue is completed, the control of that cue is moved from the 'next' fader to the 'live' fader, allowing a new cue to be loaded to the 'next' fader.

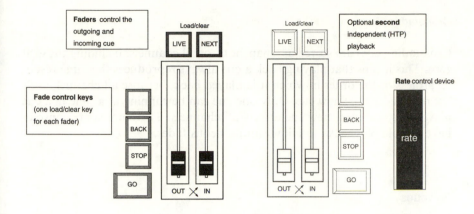

Figure 8.10 Example of preset-oriented playbacks with cue faders

In some consoles the manual faders don't control the 'live' and 'blind' scenes; instead they control the up-fading and down-fading channels between the 'live' and 'next' cues. The main difference is that cues are loaded or cleared to the whole playback (not each fader). Once the transition to a new cue is completed the faders no longer control that cue; instead they control the up-fading and down-fading channels in the transition to the next cue.

If there are several cue playbacks, they interact on a highest takes precedence basis, as if they were duplicate systems addressing the same channels simultaneously (see Fig. 4.2).

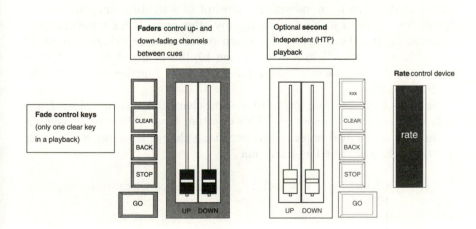

Figure 8.11 Example of preset-oriented playbacks with up-/down-faders

Crossfades

Crossfading cues are stored as 'snapshots' of all channels, including those at zero. This means that playing back a cue always reproduces the same result, regardless of the order in which it is played back, because all channel levels are replaced by the new cue. Only one cue can be running at a time in a cue playback since every new cue affects all channels. Therefore some consoles have double playbacks to allow simultaneous fades.

Part cues

Some consoles allow a cue to be split up into several parts, each with a fade time of its own. The total time of the cue is equal to the sum of the longest fade and delay times (see Figure 8.8).

Allfades

Consoles with two cue playbacks often have a special cue for automatically fading both to a new cue. This is called an Allfade.

Editing crossfading cues

A crossfading cue is an individual snapshot of a lighting state that can be edited and updated without affecting any other cues. If the same change is required in several subsequent cues (such as, for example, bringing channel 1 down from full to 60% in cues 1 through 10) this change has to be done in all of those cues. Some consoles have a special function for this called Record Track.

Shown below are four crossfades. The channel levels are plotted and stored individually in every cue. This does not have to be time consuming if the cues are plotted sequentially, because a change is simply made to the previous cue and stored as a new cue.

	Channel 1	Channel 2	Channel 3	Channel 4
Cue 1	FF	0	0	0
Cue 2	FF	50	30	0
Cue 3	FF	50	0	0
Cue 4	80	30	0	75

Example: Playing back crossfading cues
These cues always provide the same result on stage even if they are faded out of order. For example, fading in cue 3 on an empty stage will produce the following result:

	Channel 1	Channel 2	Channel 3	Channel 4
Cue 3	FF	50	0	0

Example: Editing a crossfading cue
If you change a channel level in a crossfading cue this will only affect that cue. If you want to alter the level of a channel through a series of cues, you have to do this in every single cue. In the next example channel 1 is modified to 75% in cue 1:

	Channel 1	Channel 2	Channel 3	Channel 4
Cue 1	<u>75</u>	0	0	0
Cue 2	FF	50	30	0
Cue 3	FF	50	0	0
Cue 4	80	30	0	75

As you can see this only affects channel 1 in cue 1.

Example: Using Record Track
The Record Track function 'tracks' a recorded change into subsequent cues, which is similar to the way cues are edited in a tracking console. This provides a possibility to edit a range of cues at the same time. The next example shows how changing channel 4 to 60% in cue 1 using Record Track will affect the following cues:

	Channel 1	Channel 2	Channel 3	Channel 4
Cue 1	75	0	0	<u>60</u>
Cue 2	FF	50	30	<u>60</u>
Cue 3	FF	50	0	<u>60</u>
Cue 4	80	30	0	75

The change was tracked and recorded as new levels for channel 4 in subsequent cues until a new level for channel 4 was encountered in cue 4.

Group fading playbacks

The philosophy of a group fading playback is the same as in a manual two-scene desk with group faders. New cues will either replace the 'live' cue completely with a crossfade, or just move a group of channels to new levels with a move fade. Normally a playback consists of function keys and two faders. During manual fades one fader controls the up-fading channels and one the down-fading channels between the 'live' and 'next' cues. Cues are loaded or cleared to the whole playback (not each fader). Once the transition to a new cue is completed the faders no longer control that cue; instead they control the up-fading and down-fading channels for the transition to the next cue.

If there are several cue playbacks, they may address the same output scene (LTP) or they may address a scene each and interact on an HTP basis.

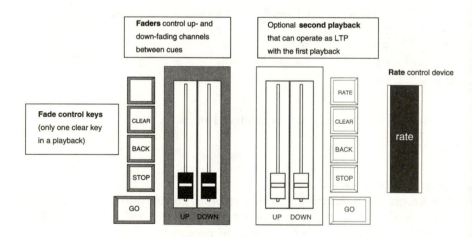

Figure 8.12 Example of group fading playbacks

Crossfades

Cues can be stored as 'snapshots' of all channels, including those at zero. This means that playing back a crossfade always reproduces the same result, regardless of the order in which it is played back, because all channel levels are moved to the levels of the new cue. Only one crossfade can be running at a time since it affects all channels. Crossfades are edited just like crossfading cues in a preset-oriented playback.

Move fades

Move-fading cues only store channels changing to a new level. When they are faded they will affect only those channels, leaving all other channels unaffected as if they were 'transparent'. The advantage of this is that several fades can run simultaneously with independent time bases (starting and ending points). When multiple move fades are operating at the same time, a crossfading cue can be used to interrupt all ongoing moves and bring all channels to a 'snapshot' state. Move fades do not produce the same result if they are faded out of order, since they affect only some channels. Editing a move fade affects subsequent cues (see examples).

Example: Move fade
When a move fading cue is started it will affect only the channels stored to a new level in that cue; other channels in previous cues that are still fading will not be affected.

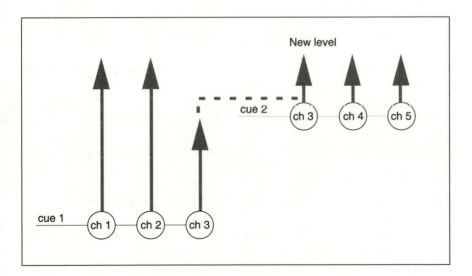

Figure 8.13 Example of a move fade with channel 3 'common'

Allfades

Consoles with two cue playbacks that interact on an HTP basis often have a special cue for automatically fading both to a new cue. This is called an Allfade.

Hard zeros

If a channel is supposed to fade out in a move-fading cue it has to be stored as 'on at 0%' as opposed to being 'transparent' (no change). This is also called a 'hard zero'.

In the following example channel 3 is stored with a hard zero in cue 3.

	Channel 1	Channel 2	Channel 3	Channel 4	
Cue 1	FF	–	–	–	
Cue 2	–	50	30	–	
Cue 3	–	–	0̲	–	< hard zero
Cue 4	80	30	–	75	

If these cues are played back sequentially this is what would happen:

Cue 1	Channel 1	Channel 2	Channel 3	Channel 4
Stage	FF			

(Channel 1 fades up to full)

Cue 2	Channel 1	Channel 2	Channel 3	Channel 4
Stage	(FF)	50	30	

(Channel 1 will stay at 100%, because no new level is assigned to it. Channel 2 moves to 50% and channel 3 to 30%)

Cue 3	Channel 1	Channel 2	Channel 3	Channel 4
Stage	(FF)	(50)	0	

(Channel 1 stays at 100%, channel 2 at 50% and channel 3 is faded out to 0%)

Cue 4	Channel 1	Channel 2	Channel 3	Channel 4
Stage	80	30	(0)	75

(Channel 1 moves to 80%, channel 2 stays at 30% channel 3 at 0% and channel 4 moves to 75%)

Example: Playing back move fades out of order
If the output is cleared and cue 3 is faded in on an empty stage the result will be a blackout, because cue 3 only contains a move for channel 3 to 0% (unless the console automatically recalculates and reproduces cue 3 as if played sequentially).

Cue 3	Channel 1	Channel 2	Channel 3	Channel 4
Stage	–	–	0	–

Editing move fades

If you change a channel level in a move-fading cue this will affect subsequent cues during sequential playback. In the next example channel 1 is modified to 75% in cue 1. If the cues are played back sequentially channel 1 will be at 75% in cues 1–3. This is a result of the 'transparency' of move-fading cues.

	Channel 1	Channel 2	Channel 3	Channel 4
Cue 1	75	–	–	–
Cue 2	–	50	30	–
Cue 3	–	–	0	–
Cue 4	80	30	–	75

Tracking playbacks

The concept of a tracking cue playback involves an approach to editing and playing back cues based on sequential shows, with multiple automated (group) fades running in the same scene. Manual fades are unusual in situations where tracking playbacks are normally used (as in Broadway shows, for example) but there are controls for taking manual control of automated fades, because a playback can have up to eight physical faders to which cues are assigned when they are started.

Besides the eight physical faders there may be up to a hundred 'virtual' faders for simultaneous fades. Each fader is like a group fader addressing channels within the same scene, which means that several cues can run simultaneously, but a channel can only be controlled by one cue fader

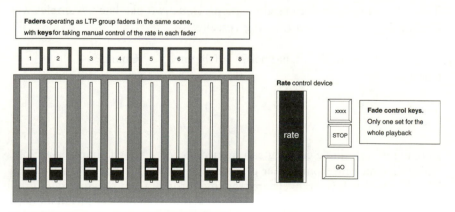

Figure 8.14 Example of a tracking playback

(physical or virtual) at a time. When a new cue is started it is automatically 'assigned' to the next unoccupied fader (or fader pair if it has split fade times). The fader(s) moves those channels only during the fade, after which they are 'released' from the fader and ready for a new 'move'.

'Tracking' fades

Technically speaking, all fades are move fades, but this fact is more or less 'hidden' from the operator, because cues either affect only some channels (normal 'tracking' fades) or all channels (block cues). Tracking fades combine the advantages of both crossfades and move fades. If a new cue is started while another is fading, common channels will be transferred to that last cue while other channels will finish in their original fade time, which is the 'transparency' advantage of move fades. Once both cues are completed the end result on stage will always be that of the last cue, because if cues are run out of order the console will recalculate all skipped moves and produce the 'right' end result on stage, which is the advantage of crossfades.

All manual

This is a special function for halting all running fades and assigning them to the rate control so they can be completed manually, which allows manual interaction over all cues running in the cue playback.

Cue sheet

This is how the same cues used in the previous two playback examples will look in the cue sheet of a tracking console.

	Channel 1	Channel 2	Channel 3	Channel 4
Cue 1	FF	–	–	–
Cue 2	(FF)	50	30	–
Cue 3	(FF)	(50)	0	–
Cue 4	80	30	–	75

Looking at any single cue you can immediately see which channels are off, which are tracking from earlier cues and which are moving to a new level. The channel levels in brackets are tracking through from previous cues until they are assigned a new level. A colour code is used to display this in modern tracking consoles; this is an example from a Strand Light Palette:

Magenta   Channel level is higher than previous cue
Green   Channel level is lower than previous cue
Blue   Channel level is unchanged (tracking) from previous cue

Unfortunately not all tracking consoles use the same colours; these are the colours in an ETC Obsession:

Blue   Channel level is higher than previous cue
Green   Channel level is lower than previous cue
Magenta   Channel level is unchanged (tracking) from previous cue

When viewed in a cue sheet this colour information provides a visual representation of the 'flow' of level changes that will take place during sequential playback.

Editing in a tracking console

When a channel(s) has to be changed in a cue the change is normally tracked into subsequent cues. In the following example channel 1 is changed to 75% in cue 1:

	Channel 1	Channel 2	Channel 3	Channel 4
Cue 1	75	–	–	–
Cue 2	(75)	50	30	–
Cue 3	(75)	(50)	0	–
Cue 4	80	30	–	75

As you can see, the level change in cue 1 of channel 1 to 75% automatically tracks through subsequent cues until it reaches a previously registered level change to 80% in cue 4. The advantage is that if you want to change the level of a channel in a series of cues, you only have to edit the first cue where that channel is to change. This is a fundamental characteristic of a tracking system. Most non-tracking consoles can edit cues in a similar way through a Record Track function.

'Cue only' recording

If a change in a cue isn't supposed to affect the subsequent cues, a 'cue only' recording can be made. This will store changes made in that cue and make the next cue a new starting point for levels tracking from the previous cue.

In the following example cue 1 will be changed and rerecorded as a cue only. Channels 1 and 4 will be set to 80%.

Before changing cue 1 and storing as cue only:

	Channel 1	Channel 2	Channel 3	Channel 4
Cue 1	75	–	–	–
Cue 2	(75)	50	30	–
Cue 3	(75)	(50)	0	–
Cue 4	80	30	–	75

After changing cue 1 and storing as cue only:

	Channel 1	Channel 2	Channel 3	Channel 4	
Cue 1	80	–	–	80	< Cue only
Cue 2	75	50	30	0	< New tracking levels
Cue 3	(75)	(50)	0	–	
Cue 4	80	30	–	75	

Blocking cues

A block cue will store all channels as specific levels (as cue only) and set all unused channels to 0%, basically making it a crossfading cue. This is useful in two ways:

• To stop levels from tracking through that cue.
• To create an absolute cue which will affect all channels, like a crossfade.

Before storing cue 3 as a block cue:

	Channel 1	Channel 2	Channel 3	Channel 4
Cue 1	FF	–	–	–
Cue 2	(FF)	50	–	–
Cue 3	(FF)	(50)	30	–
Cue 4	(FF)	(50)	(30)	75
Cue 5	(FF)	(50)	0	(75)

After storing cue 3 as a block cue:

	Channel 1	Channel 2	Channel 3	Channel 4	
Cue 1	FF	–	–	–	
Cue 2	(FF)	50	–	–	
Cue 3 B	FF	50	30	0	< Block cue
Cue 4	(FF)	(50)	(30)	75	
Cue 5	(FF)	(50)	0	(75)	

Channels 1–3 are now tracking from cue 3, any changes made to, for example, channel 1 in cue 1 will not track through to cue 3 or 4. Also, channel 4 was set to zero so any changes in previous cues are guaranteed not to track past cue 3. Individual channels can be blocked too. A block cue is often used at the beginning and end of an act.

Example: Playing back tracking cues
As mentioned earlier, cues can be faded out of order because the console will scan backwards through all moves and reproduce a cue as if faded in order.

Fading in cue 3 from this cue sheet:

	Channel 1	Channel 2	Channel 3	Channel 4
Cue 1	FF	–	–	–
Cue 2	(FF)	50	–	–
Cue 3	(FF)	(50)	30	–
Cue 4	80	30	(30)	75

will produce this result:

Cue 3	(FF)	(50)	30	(0)

9 Effects

The term 'effect' in a lighting context is subjective, and can apply to anything from bumping individual channels manually to playing back a complex pattern of some sort. A sequence of cues looped with a link from the last cue to the first, and played back in a cue playback, is one way of creating a sequential effect (see 'The order in which cues can be stored' in Chapter 8), but most consoles have separate functions for creating and playing back effects.

In its simplest form an effect is a loop (or 'stack') of 'looks' that are advanced automatically in a pattern of some sort. An effect can also be called a chase or a sequence. Some consoles play back effects as cues in the cue playbacks, some play back effects from submasters or from special effect masters. The capacity of a console for quickly creating effect patterns and affecting how they are played back varies a lot. Traditionally, 'live' consoles have pretty extensive effect functions since they may be a substantial component in the design. There are consoles that can trig the speed of an effect to a sound input, or a MIDI timing clock that provides 'beats per second', which is how the tempo of a song is often categorized. This chapter can only hint at the different functions that exist for creating effects, since this is one of the features that varies most between consoles.

Direction of an effect

An effect is basically a list of memories or channels played back sequentially. Usually there are different modes affecting the direction of an effect.

- *Forward*
A list of memories is played forwards sequentially.

- *Back*
The direction of an effect is reversed.

- *Bounce*
The direction of an effect is alternated back/forward.

- *Step*

Each effect step is advanced manually to synchronize with the performance.

Additive or subtractive

Usually an effect is played back adding intensities from each step to the output, but sometimes it may be set to subtract levels for channels already lit.

Transitions between steps

There are different transitions between effect steps, that may be set as a general mode for the whole effect, or individually for each step. Each mode provides a different 'character' to the effect. The times for an effect may be individual up/down and delay times for each step, or a fixed time for how long each step 'holds' before the next step.

- *Soft/soft*

The effect fades between steps.

- *Soft/hard*

The effect fades in and cuts out.

- *Hard/hard*

The effect cuts between steps; usually the step time is how long each step is 'on'.

- *Hard/soft*

The effect cuts in and fades out.

Transitions between effects

When an effect is played back from a submaster it can be faded in and out manually. Some consoles can define times for how an effect fades in, holds and fades out when an effect is played back from a submaster or as an effect cue.

NOTE: When an effect is played back as a cue in a tracking console like the ETC Obsession, the channels in the effect are not controlled by any physical fader once the effect has faded in. This means that the effect will only stop when a new cue is started addressing those channels.

Sound control of an effect

There are a variety of means by which the light of an effect can be synchronized with sound. These are a few:

- *'Light organ'*
Some consoles have a 'light organ' input that allows different frequency ranges of a sound source to affect submasters or memories directly (bass = memory 1, low mid = memory 2, high mid = memory 3, treble = memory 4).

- *'Bass trig'*
Sometimes bass frequencies of a sound source are used, for example, to advance the steps of a chase.

Rate control of an effect

Usually the total speed of an effect can be speeded up or slowed down. The change may be expressed as a relative value in per cent or as an absolute value in the form of beats per second.

- *Tap*
A very useful function for adapting the speed of an effect to a musical theme is a 'tap' function, which allows the operator to tap a tempo on a button, which will set the speed of the effect.

10   Macro functions

A macro is a function for grouping a sequence of commands so that they can be executed with a single command. Macros allow the operator to customize frequently used combinations of functions to speed up programming and simplify playback operations. Macros can be trigged in different ways depending on the console; for example they can be activated with a key, a MIDI command, a contact closure (external trig input), a submaster or linked to a cue. This makes macros a good way of incorporating lighting consoles in a show control environment, allowing other devices to trig functions in the console.

Since a macro is a list of functions in a specific console it will only provide the same result in that console. In the examples in this chapter the console each macro applies to is specified, but the principle is the same in all consoles.

Macros for programming

Macros can be useful for playing back regularly-used sequences of commands during plotting and rehearsals such as, for example, 'set all lights to zero, light the worklights and load the first cue of act 2 to the playbacks again'. Macros can also be used for editing cues when a repetitive command such as 'take down channel 5 and 6 and set channel 25 to full' needs to be implemented in a lot of different cues.

Example: Channel check macro (ETC Expression)
This is a common macro in boards that don't have a function for checking channels one by one during focusing. The functions 'AT 00 NEXT AT FULL' are put together in a macro. Selecting a channel at full to check and activating this macro will set that channel to 00; step to the next channel and set it at full. Stepping to the next channel after this is done by repeating the macro, etc. Another macro can be used for stepping to the previous channel instead of the next.

Macro wait times

Some boards allow macros to have wait times (MACRO WAIT) between functions, and a looping to auto-repeat the macro when done, which opens up even more possibilities.

Example: Channel auto-check macro (ETC Expression)
The previous macro is expanded with a wait time and a repeat loop into 'AT 00 NEXT AT FULL MACRO WAIT 6 M(x)' where (x) is the number of the same macro, so it loops back to itself after 6 seconds. This macro will set the currently selected channel at 0%, set the next channel to full, wait 6 seconds and then repeat the procedure stepping to the next channel, etc.

Controlling moving lights (Avolites)

Some moving lights can execute subroutines programmed into the fixture (for example, resetting the fixture) when a certain combination of DMX levels are sent to the fixture. Some consoles with support for moving lights, like the Avolites Rolacue, provide factory set-up macros to send these commands. These subroutines may be supported in other ways in other consoles.

Macros for playback

A macro can be useful to solve a combination of events that should be trigged during playback, such as 'load submaster page 4 and start effect 3'. Macros are also useful for remote controlling functions in a lighting console through MIDI or some other interface, for example MIDI Show Control (FIRE macro) (see 'MIDI and time code' in Chapter 18).

Example: Run cue 3 (Strand GeniusPlus software)
A macro consisting of 'CUE 20 GO' can be used to run cue 20 from a single macro. This macro may be started by MIDI or linked to another cue.

Example: Run cue # and fade submaster 1 (AVAB Panther)
The macro 'GOTO START + MASTER KEY 1' will start a transition to any cue # entered previously, and fade the memory stored in submaster 1. The RPN syntax is easy to adapt to this kind of 'selectable' macro, since all functions start with a number. This macro may be trigged from the external input (contact closure) or MIDI.

11 Storing and printing shows

When a show has been programmed into the memory of a console it is useful to be able to store that information in a 'long-term' memory storage medium, like a floppy diskette. This means that the console can be used for working on more than one production, and that the show can be transferred to another console. It is a safety measure backing up the 'show data' if the console should break down. It's also the best 'undo' function in the world if a show has been accidentally altered by some advanced editing function, because the 'previous version' can be downloaded back into the memory of the console.

Floppy diskette drive

The most common format for storing data today is the 3.5″ high density floppy diskette, which is used for light consoles, personal computers, synthesizers and most other computer applications. It's small, cheap, practical and relatively fast.

Figure 11.1 Floppy HD diskette

● *Formatting diskettes*

Before a diskette can be used it has to be formatted to the system it is being used in. The formatting procedure prepares the diskette for the information that will be stored and is done only once. Disks can be bought preformatted for different standard formats. A standard format for IBM-compatible personal computers is DOS-format, which many light consoles are compatible with today.

● *Handling diskettes*

A floppy diskette is a magnetic medium, like a cassette. This means that it is sensitive to magnetic fields and should not be placed on top of monitors or loudspeakers, since they transmit these kinds of fields. Diskettes can be put through X-ray machines at airports but should not be taken through the metal detector, since this device operates using a magnetic field. They should not be exposed to excess heat in the form of direct sunlight, or humidity.

Hard disk drive (HDD)

A hard disk will allow you to store information much in the same way as a floppy, but much more and faster. This means hundreds of shows can be stored, along with macros and other user data. A hard disk is usually built into a console.

Memory card

A memory card is the size of a credit card, with the advantage that the drive for it is very small and easy to incorporate in a design at low cost. It is quick to read and write to but the actual cards are expensive compared to a floppy and require a small battery to maintain memory intact.

Compatibility between consoles

A show saved on, for example, a floppy diskette in one console cannot be loaded straight into another console, because they do not read the show data of the diskette in the same way. This means they are not compatible. There is a standard format for reading and writing light data as an ASCII text file that has been designed to overcome this problem (see 'Standard ASCII Light Cues').

Printing a show

Many lighting consoles will allow you to print your show data. This is useful for documentation of a show. In larger theatre consoles you can choose between different printing formats, depending on whether you want to print only the patch, or the sequence, or cues 1–40.

Part 3 – Console Features for Specific Lighting Devices

Introduction

Lighting consoles are mainly used to control three kinds of lighting devices.

- dimmers, for conventional lights
- scrollers
- moving lights.

To understand certain functions in a console it is necessary to understand the features of each lighting device that the console is designed to control. A basic understanding of DMX512 (Chapter 16) is also required, because that is how the console is communicating to these devices. These chapters look into the basic aspects of controlling dimmers, scrollers and moving lights.

12 Dimmers

Basically, dimmers have been functioning by the same principles of phase control since 1947 (see Chapter 1). Each half of the AC waveform is passed though a device that works like a 'gate' which opens up to let a 'portion' of the waveform through, and then closes. This 'chopping' process is done 50 to 60 times a second, which results in a regulated average voltage (open gate = full output). The 'gate' device receives a control signal from the lighting console that describes how much of the waveform it should let through, expressed as a value between 0 and 100%.

The first gates were electronic twin valve thyratron tubes, which were fairly expensive and somewhat unstable. In 1959 they were replaced by solid state 'valves' in the form of a pair of silicon-controlled rectifiers (SCRs), also called thyristors or triacs. With the SCRs dimmers could be made that were compact, stable and economical. In the 1970s the ramp that trigged the SCRs was designed to trig from a digital signal instead of an analogue voltage reference, which gave a more precise control of the dimming ramp, but the 'AC chopping' mechanism remained unchanged. Even if only the ramp is digital these dimmers are often called 'digital dimmers'. Lately other types of solid state gate devices (transistors) are being used which can be applied in a way that produces less electrical noise. This technology is still quite new, but it doesn't change any of the information in this chapter, because from a control point of view there will always be a control signal that is sent to the dimmer explaining how it should regulate the output to the lights.

DMX address

A dimmer has to be given a unique address corresponding to a control channel in the lighting console, and usually a dimmer with several dimmer channels only requires the address to be set for the first dimmer channel. If you are using DMX512, this address will be a DMX output number 1–512, which means that a 12-channel dimmer with the DMX address 1 will respond to control channels 1–12. If two dimmers should operate simultaneously they can be set to the same address or they can be patched to the

Figure 12.1 Dimmer cabinet (Courtesy Strand Lighting)

same control channel in the lighting console (see Chapter 5). The latter is preferable because the control signal to each dimmer can be controlled from the lighting console, allowing one to be unpatched if there is a malfunction.

Different response curves

The way the output of a dimmer corresponds to a linear fade (0–100%) is called the dimming response curve of that dimmer. Early thyristor dimmers produced a slightly S-shaped dimming response curve from zero to full, related to the sinoidal waveform of the AC. With this S-shaped curve, most lights would be 'slow' in the bottom and top parts of a fade. This may be desirable in some situations, but in modern dimmers this S-curve is

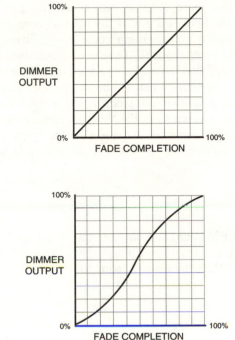

Figure 12.2 Linear

Figure 12.3 Sinus

usually compensated to give a linear response instead (see Figures 12.2 and 12.3).

It may be desirable to use different response curves, depending on the light source being controlled and the situation.

- Light sources react differently to dimming, for example a 2000 W light will start fading in later than a 500 W light, which can be compensated with a 'fast bottom' curve for the 2000 W light.
- In television a dimming curve that is faster in the bottom part of the fade, providing a 'distinct blackout', is often preferred, while for theatre lighting, overall intensities are lower in general, and a more precise control over the bottom of a fade is required.

Defining a dimmer response curve

In some dimmers different predefined curves (also called profiles or dimmer laws) can be selected, so that a linear input from the lighting console will produce a different dimmer response. The advantage of this is that any lighting console can be used, but the dimmer curves cannot be edited and stored to a show in the board. Another way of achieving different response curves is to change the linear output of the lighting console.

The DMX512 signal from a lighting console is a linear stream of data from 0 to 100% for each channel. The 'real' resolution of the signal is higher, 256 steps from 0–100% (0–255 = 8 bits), but these steps are usually not displayed to the operator. When a dimmer receives a DMX value for a channel it trigs the dimming circuit according to a conversion table in the dimmer. This is often referred to as the 'internal resolution' of the dimmer, and usually there are thousands of steps so that the 'gaps' between the 256 DMX bits are filled in smoothly by the dimmer during fades.

Linear

A true linear response in board and dimmer may not seem 'linear' to the eye. For some light sources the perceived linear change in intensity from 50% to full is less noticeable than the change from 50% to zero.

S-curve

An S-curve will produce a slow bottom and top fade; this is the 'original' curve of an analogue thyristor dimmer.

Square law

A curve with a slow bottom and fast top fade is called 'square law' because it is a result of dividing the dimmer travel into ten equal steps from 0 to 100% and making the output follow the square of each step number (Figure 12.4).

Step	Linear %	Square %
0	0	0
1	10	1
2	20	4
3	30	9
4	40	16
5	50	25
6	60	36
7	70	49
8	80	64
9	90	81
10	100	100

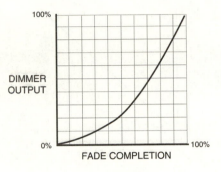

Figure 12.4 Square

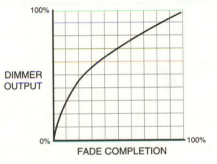

Figure 12.5 Inverted square

Inverted square law

A fast-bottom and slow-top dimmer curve equal to an inverted square law is sometimes called a 'television' curve. It provides a definite fade-out at the bottom of the fade, and fine control over the top part of the fade which corresponds to the response of the cameras. It is also useful to compensate the slow fade response of high wattage lights (Figure 12.5).

Preheat at #%

A dimmer curve that starts at, for example, 4% instead of 0% will preheat any light source to that level at all times (Figure 12.6).

Non-dim (full at %)

If a non-dimmable instrument such as a follow spot or smoke machine is connected to a dimmer so it can be controlled from the console, the dimmer

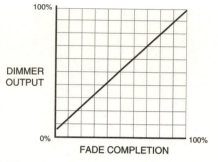

Figure 12.6 Preheat at 4%

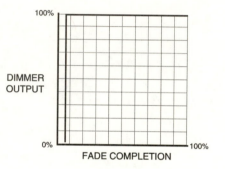

Figure 12.7 Non-dim

should be set to a nondim curve to prevent dimming of the device. This curve will switch the dimmer to full at a specified level of, for example, 4% and may also be called a relay curve (Figure 12.7).

Continuous

A continuous dimmer curve is set to full at all levels, which means the intensity will be 100% at all times. This may also be called a 'hot patch' (Figure 12.8).

Fluorescent and neon

Fluorescent and neon lights can be dimmed just like conventional lights but there are some important differences. Since they are discharge lamps with no physical connection between live and neutral they require a ballast, and a dimmer curve with a voltage 'burst' at the bottom of the fade to initiate the discharge process. This is not a rule though, there are also electronic ballasts that can dim directly and that are controlled with 0–10 V (Figure 12.9).

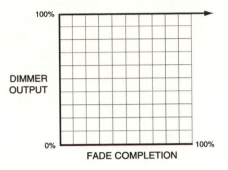

Figure 12.8 Continuous

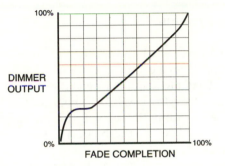

Figure 12.9 Fluorescent

120 V in 230 V dimmer: WARNING!

It may seem a good idea to have a 230 V dimmer control 120 V equipment by limiting the output, because if the highest level of the response curve is set to 50% this would theoretically mean that the dimmer will output 120 V. This is not entirely true, because even if the 'medium' (RMS) output will measure 120 V, the amplitude 'peaks' are still 230 V (Figure 12.10). The following are some good precautions to keep in mind:

- Light bulbs specified for 120 V will function with this curve, although the lamp hours will probably be reduced due to the transients. Apart from lamps, no 120 V equipment should ever be powered in this way.
- The lamp housing must be rated for 230 V. It is dangerous to use a luminaire rated for 120 V, such as US PAR cans, for example. The same applies to two 120 V spotlights wired in series and connected to a 230 V linear curve.
- A thyristor or triac fault may cause the dimmer to go to full despite the curve, blowing any connected 120 V lights.

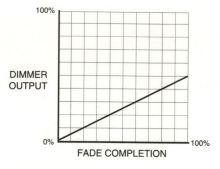

Figure 12.10 120 V for 230 V dimmer

Dimmer monitoring systems

A dimmer monitoring system is a link reporting dimmer status back to the lighting console. This provides a central overview of a large and distributed dimmer installation to facilitate maintenance and isolating faults. There are two pins in the specification of the DMX512 connector that may be used for this (see 'DMX512 – a revolution!', Chapter 16), but most manufacturers use a proprietary data link back to the board (ETCNet, Strand ShowNet and AVABNet, for example).

Dimmer monitoring systems can display information from the dimmers directly onto the screen of the lighting console, or in a separate system. The type and amount of information you can monitor varies from system to system, but the following are examples of things that can be reported:

- if the mains power feeding the dimmer rack is faulty (voltage/phasing/ frequency)
- if there are temperature problems
- if a breaker has tripped
- if a load is missing (possible lamp failure)
- if there is a faulty data (DMX) line
- if a dimmer has faulted (thyristor or triac problem, for example).

The types of dimmer errors that can be reported vary from system to system; this is an extract from an ETCLink system (1996):

DIMMER STATUS
Dimmer label: Stage left
Channel: 2
Proportion: 100
Profile: 0

Console dimmer level: 54
Parked: no
Rack/slot number: 1/1
Rack dimmer level: 54
Dimmer level source: DMX A
Recorded lamp load: 700 W
Load at full: 700 W
Actual load: 0 W
Boost: –
Dimmer errors: none

Fatal or secondary messages

Fatal messages deal with anything that could potentially terminate or drastically change the look of a show; secondary messages are less critical and deal with individual dimmer problems and warnings of potential rack temperature problems.

Examples of fatal messages

- Dimmer # has shut down due to an over-temperature condition. The dimmer will remain shut down until the condition is cleared at the dimmer rack.
- Rack # DMX port A/B failure. Either there is a problem with the DMX cabling/connections between the console and the rack, or the rack has been configured incorrectly.
- Rack # A/B/C phase input (main) voltage is in error at # V.
- Rack # input (main) frequency is out of spec. at # Hz.
- ETCLink (the feedback connection) has failed. Please check cabling and connections. If the problem persists, please call a certified technician.
- Rack # processor error.

Examples of secondary messages

- Dimmer # has a load but the recorded load is zero. Because the recorded load is zero the dimmer monitoring system is unable to determine whether the dimmer has a load error.
- The load on dimmer # has changed. Because the dimmer output is not at a high enough level, the dimmer monitoring system is unable to determine the size of the load.
- The load on dimmer # has changed from # watts to # watts. A decreased load indicates lamp failure. An increased load indicates that a lamp has been added since the load was recorded last.

- DC output has been detected on dimmer #. If this condition persists it may harm the connected load. Please check the connected load.
- An SCR has failed on/off in dimmer #. The dimmer should be replaced.
- Dimmer # output has failed on. The dimmer should be replaced.
- Dimmer # output has failed off. Either the circuit breaker has tripped or the dimmer needs to be replaced.
- Dimmer #'s load has failed. The most likely cause is a lamp failure. Either replace the lamp or, to prevent further error messages, clear the load.
- Rack # ambient temperature is high at # degrees Fahrenheit. The temperature does not yet exceed acceptable operational limits, but the rack should be checked. Please check the cooling/ventilation in the dimmer room.
- Rack # ambient temperature is low at # degrees Fahrenheit. Please check the cooling/ventilation in the dimmer room.
- Rack # ambient temperature is outside the acceptable operational range at # degrees Fahrenheit. Please check the cooling/ventilation in the dimmer room immediately.
- The phasing in rack # is not allowed. The rack has been shut down. Please check the input power service.

13   Scrollers

A scroller is a colour changer that fits into the filter holder of a lighting instrument. Basically, a selection of colour gels is joined with heat-resistant tape, and mounted on two rolls that are motorized. When the motor receives a control signal from the lighting console it will 'scroll' the gel roll until the desired filter is in place.

Controlling a scroller

Scrollers are usually designed to be controlled by the standard output from lighting consoles (to dimmers) to make it simple to incorporate them with existing equipment. Early scrollers were controlled by analogue control (0– 10 V), but today almost only DMX512 is used. DMX512 was not designed to control scrollers, but most boards have found ways to integrate scrollers with conventional lights by making special software for handling scroller functions called attributes.

Attributes

A lighting instrument with a scroller is really a multichannel device, consisting of a dimmer channel, a gel roll with colour frames and maybe additional control channels for fan or speed in the scroller. The control of this multi-channel device is usually solved by assigning the scrollers functions as 'attributes' to the dimmer channel. An attribute channel is designed to recognize the requirements of the scroller function it is controlling, and handle this automatically in the control environment. Dimmer intensities are usually controlled as HTP (highest takes precedence) channels, but scroller attributes are best controlled as LTP (latest takes precedence) for two reasons.

1. So it will stay where it was last set until a new change is required, even during lighting changes concerning intensities.

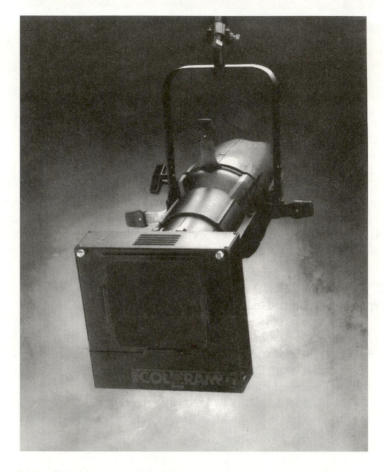

Figure 13.1 Scroller with a conventional light (Coloram, courtesy Wybron)

  2. So it is possible to override all earlier settings and select a certain gel at
     any time.

Colour attributes

There are scrollers (also called frames) that handle over 30 colours. Figure
13.2 shows how the levels 0–100% in the lighting console will correspond to
100 different positions on the gel roll. Setting the control channel to 50%
will scroll to the middle of the gel roll, and if it consists of 11 frames this will
be frame 6. Some lighting consoles give access to the full 256 steps of
DMX512 to get a higher positioning accuracy, which is necessary for scrollers controlling long gel rolls.

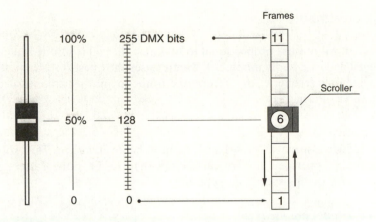

Figure 13.2 DMX control of scroller frames

Some scrollers have a special operating mode that will 'round off' to the nearest whole colour frame when a control signal is received. This is often called frame mode. The advantage is that the 'exact' control value for a colour frame won't be important, just being 'close' is enough. The disadvantage is that it won't be possible to scroll slowly from one frame to another, since the scroller will always 'jump' from one whole frame to the next whole frame (unless the scroller has DMX speed control). It also won't be possible to use 'half frames' combining two colours, since only one or the other is chosen. This is solved when a console treats a scroller as an attribute. The colour attribute is usually subdivided into the actual frames of the scroller, allowing colour 4 to be chosen as '4' instead of maybe 'level 36%', which provides a 'frame' mode in the board without having to give up the advantages of fading between frames, or selecting half frames. In some systems it is also possible to label and display each frame by name.

Fan attributes

Most scrollers have a fan to prevent saturated filters from overheating when exposed to high intensities of light for longer periods. To keep noise levels down, some scrollers have a switch to set the fan in high or low operation, or a thermostat starting the fan at certain temperatures. For shows where any noise generated by fans or other equipment is critical, it is best to use scrollers that allow the fan to be controlled from the board. This way the fan can be applied selectively to keep the noise down.

HINT: If the fan control channel is patched to the light channel, the fan will be applied proportionally to the intensity of the light of that instrument.

Speed attributes

Mechanical noise is proportional to how fast the roll is scrolled (especially if the gel rolls are badly mounted), which raises the question of how the speed at which the scroller changes from one frame to another is controlled. There are three alternatives:

1. *Internal speed*
An internal speed is preset and cannot be overridden. This solution is acceptable provided no critical change has to be done faster, and the noise level of this speed is acceptable.

2. *Fade times are used*
The change is executed in the fade time of the colour control channel. This means that the speed will be relative to how many frames are changed, because fading from frame 1 to 4 in 4 seconds is a speed of 1 frame per second, while fading from frame 1 to 8 in the same time is twice as fast (2 frames per second).

3. *Speed attribute*
The scroller uses an internal speed parameter that can be controlled from the lighting console. This way the speed can be applied selectively, and will probably provide smoother fading at slower speeds.

Scrollers in submasters

Submasters that handle both HTP dimmer intensities and LTP scrollers or moving lights can treat LTP channels in three ways:

1. As soon as a submaster is moved, scrollers will jump to the control of that submaster. This is a pretty unpractical solution because you have to keep track of where your scrollers were last controlled from, so that moving a submaster won't send them reeling to a new colour.
2. As soon as a submaster is moved under a specified level (10%, for example), scrollers will jump to the control of that master. This behaviour allows you to decide when you want a submaster to gain control of the scroller's channels.
3. The submaster fader will control intensities as HTP and a key is pressed for LTP channels to jump to the control of that master. This way the control of scroller channels can be transferred from one master to another without affecting dimmer intensities.

Scrollers in cue playbacks

During sequential playback of cues, a scroller is usually set to a colour, and remains through subsequent cues until a new change is required. This means that scrollers fit perfectly into the natural playback philosophy of group fading and tracking consoles where all channels are LTP in the cue playbacks.

How scrollers are programmed into cues depends on the concept of each console. The following example shows a succession of cues where a light/scroller fades out, changes colour and fades back in a console with scroller support.

In this example the scroller is an attribute to channel 1.

	Ch 1	Ch 2	Ch 3	Ch 4	
Cue 1	50%				< 1 @ 50%, frame 2
	Col 2				
Cue 2	0%				< 1 to 0%, select frame 3
	Col 3				
Cue 3	60%				< 1 to 60%, frame 3
	Col 3				

Sometimes colour changes can have separate times, and a default setting to change when the lights have faded out in the previous cue.

Rigging scrollers

Follow the instructions of each manufacturer to rig and set up a scroller. The following are some general aspects (see also Figure 16.5).

- *Control address*
Each scroller has to be given a unique address corresponding to a control channel in the lighting console. If you are using DMX512 to control the scroller this address will be a DMX channel number 1–512 that you set on the scroller (before powering up).

- *Power and control signal*
A scroller needs a control signal from the lighting console and a power feed for the motors. This is usually solved in the same cable by running the lighting console DMX through a distributor box that adds a low voltage power feed for the motors and sends the combination to the scroller.

WARNING: Make sure the power/DMX cable to the scrollers is rigged clear of warm light instrument housings. If the cable melts you may find yourself at the lighting console with the DC voltage for the scroller motors coming in on the DMX line. To prevent this, make sure there is an opto-isolator in the power distribution box for the scrollers.

- *Calibration*

Some scrollers need to calibrate when they are powered up, so the scroller can 'learn' how long the gel roll is and where the start and end frames are, and make these correspond to the lowest and highest values from the lighting console. This procedure involves scrolling from frame 1 to the last frame and back.

HINT: The most common mishap with a scroller is that the gel roll comes loose at either end, leaving the stage white and producing a flapping noise with every preprogrammed change. Be careful to assemble the gel rolls aligned, using only heat-resistant filters and heat-resistant joining tape.

- *Patch fan and speed to save control channels*

If you are controlling colour, fan and speed, you may want to patch all fan channels into one control channel and all speed channels into another control channel. This will save you a lot of control channels, but assumes that you won't need to control speed or fan individually at any time.

Two scrollers with separate colour, fan and speed control are patched.

Scroller 1 is controlled by DMX channel 401–403 and scroller 2 is controlled by DMX channel 404–406.

Scroller 1	Colour	Fan	Speed
DMX ch	401	402	403
Patch to control ch		40	41

Scroller 1	Colour	Fan	Speed
DMX ch	404	405	406
Patch to control ch		40	41

Both fans are controlled by control channel 40 and both speeds by control channel 41. Putting these two channels on two submasters (for example) gives you manual control for these parameters throughout the performance.

Designing with scrollers

Using scrollers in a lighting design requires careful planning. Once you know what filters you will be using in your design you can start planning the gel rolls. Be sure of your colour choices, as adding a colour frame to a taped gel roll already mounted in a scroller is quite tricky. If you are uncertain, you can add some alternative filter choices to the gel roll. Plan colours that will be involved in succession close to each other in the gel roll to avoid unnecessary scrolling. You will need a 'blank' frame to get white light. If you put this as the first frame you will get white light when the control channel is at 0%, and if you put it in the middle you will get a minimum distance from white to any colour frame.

Prepare colour groups

You can save yourself some programming time by preparing colour groups. This way you can quickly select and change a setting for large combinations of scrollers using the group functions of the lighting console.

Group 1: Backlight scrollers
Group 2: Frontlight scrollers
Group 3: Sidelight left scrollers
Group 4: Sidelight right scrollers
Group 5: All scrollers in the rig

Now you can select, for example, all scrollers except the backlight scrollers by selecting group 5 'minus' group 1.

Have a start-up cue for the show

Record frames for every scroller in a starting cue before the first light cue of the show so you know they are positioned right every time the show begins.

Have a 'zero positioning' cue

Store a cue or memory with all scrollers on white so they can all be reset and checked at the beginning of a show.

14 Moving lights

A moving light is a light source in which not only intensity can be controlled, but also parameters controlling the direction and character of the beam. Sometimes moving lights are referred to as 'intelligent fixtures', but most of the 'intelligence' involved in controlling a moving light is required at the control end, which is the console (and the operator). There are two main types of moving lights:

- moving yokes
- moving mirrors.

Moving yokes

A moving yoke is basically a light fixture which is physically mounted in a motorized yoke which uses motors to move, pan and tilt up to 270°/360°. There are concepts such as the VL5 (Vari*Lite) or the StudioColor (High End), which are high-performance fixtures for 'concert lighting', with fixtures that can alter colour and shape of the beam, and there are motorized yokes that can be fitted with a range of conventional lights for remote refocusing in theatre and television such as, for example, the Conductor (AVAB) or the Strand PALS series. Moving yokes are preferable if a conventional 'wash' type of light like that of a PAR can or a fresnel is required, because this kind of light is best projected from a fixture instead of a mirror. The aesthetics of the moving fixture may have a value of its own in some situations, but the mechanical impetus of moving the whole fixture usually limits the acceleration times that can be used with a moving yoke. This aspect is easier to control in a moving mirror.

Moving mirrors

Moving mirrors originated in the disco lighting industry as effect projectors with an 'animated beam'. Today there are impressive beasts like the Cyberlight (High End), the Super Scan (Clay Paky) or the PAL 1200

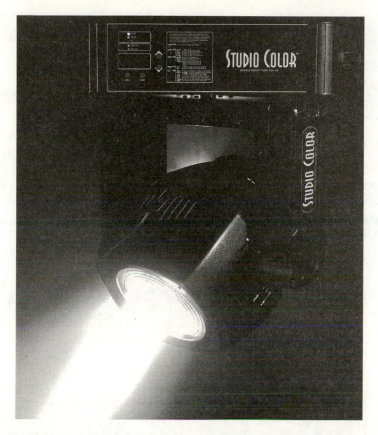

Figure 14.1 Moving yoke (Studiocolor, courtesy High End)

(Martin) which have a 'symphony of features' that can be used to create different results in concert, theatre and television applications. Unlike a moving yoke, only the beam is redirected, using a small motorized mirror. Before the beam hits the mirror it passes through an optical 'train' where different mechanical and optical devices such as dicroid (glass) colour filters and gobos are put in the path of the beam to create effects. A mirror has a much smaller range of movement than a yoke, the radius for pan and tilt rarely exceed 110°/170°, but there are certain mechanical advantages to a mirror. Since only the small mirror is moved, acceleration times can be anything from a 'snap' change to a slow ramp. The possible speeds are also much higher (around ten times) since there is almost no momentum in the mirror. The fixture doesn't require any additional 'operating space' because only the beam moves, which makes it easy to incorporate it in a cramped rig.

Figure 14.2 Optical train in a moving mirror fixture (Courtesy High End)

Figure 14.3 Moving mirror fixture (Cyberlight, courtesy High End)

Controlling a moving light

There is no standard for how a moving light should be designed or controlled. Nowadays most moving lights are controlled by DMX512, so even if some companies still use proprietary protocols, this chapter will only deal with DMX devices.

A moving light is a multichannel device using several DMX output channels to control its different functions, but a moving light can also be a combination of several devices that are used simultaneously like a moving yoke with a conventional light controlled by a dimmer, plus a scroller. Every parameter may be produced by different mechanics, but they are all controlled as DMX output channels. Since every fixture has functions that can be 'played in different ways', it is of interest that the console recognizes the requirements of each control parameter in a moving light.

Attributes

The parameters of a moving light are the different functions that can be individually controlled. Treating each parameter as an attribute of a single unit is a way of grouping these parameters so they are automatically mapped to the individual control functions of the board, like trackballs and colour mixing wheels. Most console manufacturers supporting moving lights analyse the possibilities of each moving fixture and provide 'personality files' that automatically map these parameters as attributes to the functions of the board. Despite this we are at a point where a single moving light can have over 30 control parameters, and an understanding of the basic aspects of these parameters can be a great asset when trying to use them.

DMX address and offset

The DMX address is the first DMX output number to which the fixture will respond. The DMX offset is the nth DMX output number originating from the DMX address. The amount of control parameters are the attributes of a fixture; for example a Cyberlight has 20 control parameters, and will occupy DMX channels 1–20 if the DMX address is set to 1. Intensity has an offset of 18, because it is the 18th parameter in the fixture.

Since a Cyberlight uses 20 DMX channels, this means five Cyberlights require 100 DMX outputs (this can be confusing, because some manufacturers list how many fixtures a board can control, and some how many attributes).

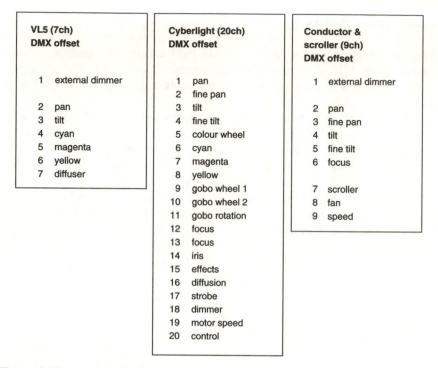

Figure 14.4 Examples of DMX offsets

Pan/tilt attributes

The fundamental parameters for controlling the movement of a light are pan and tilt. The 8-bit resolution of a DMX output channel is 256 steps from zero to full (see 'Analogue control and DMX512'). This means that the full movement of the pan and tilt parameters will be divided into 256 'steps' and for a moving light with a 360° pan this means less than a step/degree, which won't allow for fine positioning control. Some moving lights support something called 'extended DMX' or '16-bit resolution' to solve this, which means pan and tilt use two DMX channels each (coarse/fine) instead of one, which provides 65 536 steps instead of 256. Usually a board supporting extended DMX will allow the user to jump between coarse and fine positioning to allow both fast movement and fine tuning.

● *Swap/invert*
Some systems allow you to invert or swap pan and tilt channels for individual instruments so that all fixtures will move to the same direction when pan or tilt is controlled.

- *Fine tune response*

The high and low levels of pan and tilt can be scaled to vary the response of pan/tilt movement to a full movement of the positioning tool (trackball or joystick, for example).

- *Transition speeds*

Some fixtures control the movements of pan/tilt as a result of the fade times programmed in the control board for a transition, and some use an internal motor speed parameter that can be controlled from the board.

- *Positioning tools*

Once pan and tilt are set up as attributes they are usually mapped to a positioning tool of some kind, such as a trackball, joystick, wheel, mouse or graphics tablet (digitizer). Pan and tilt are traditionally referred to as the 'focus' of a moving light, which is confusing, because focus also applies to the sharpness of a lightbeam.

- *Flip*

A motorized yoke can have two pan/tilt values for every position on stage. The 'flip' function allows you to access the 'opposite' position quickly.

Intensity attributes

The 'dimming' of a moving light can either be an external dimmer feeding the lamp (as for a VL5), or if a discharge lamp is used it can be a mechanical dimmer inside the fixture (as in most mirror fixtures), providing 'full optical dimming' and hopefully a smooth fade to black. A fixture with a discharge lamp usually needs a starting pulse to fire up the lamp, and in some cases this can be mapped as an attribute or macro in the control board (see Chapter 10). Some fixtures require several parameters such as iris, shutters and colour mixing to be set to full before there is any light output. It may be simpler to invert the control channels for these parameters so that only the intensity channel requires a value to provide light.

- *Strobe*

Some mechanical dimmers, or a separate shutter, can be operated so fast that they produce a stroboscopic effect. This is sometimes controlled by the upper scale of the same DMX channel as the intensity or as a separate channel. The capacity of a strobe is usually expressed as flashes per second (FPS).

Colour attributes

There are two main solutions for changing colours in a moving light, colour wheels or colour mixing systems. Some systems offer several systems at the same time, mainly because more colours can be achieved this way.

- *Colour wheels*

The colour wheels use dicroic glass filters, which are great for saturated colours but provide a choice limited to the amount of filters. Sometimes there are two colour wheels, allowing more filters and combinations of both wheels to provide more variations. The filters are put in the optical train by a rotating wheel controlled by 'micro stepping motors' that allow rapid selection of colours. Some fixtures will only allow 'step' control of whole colours, and some allow half colours to be defined too. Usually the bottom range of the DMX channel controlling the colours will control filter selections, and the top range can be used to set the colour wheel in a continuous 'spinning' effect at variable speed. Some filters may be colour correction filters to adjust the colour temperature of the light from the fixture.

- *Colour mixing systems*

A colour mixing system can provide thousands of colours by mixing three basic colour components such as cyan, magenta and yellow. These are the same colours that are used in colour printing processes to reproduce a full colour image. Theoretically any colour can be achieved by colour mixing, but in reality really saturated deep colours are hard to achieve, because three

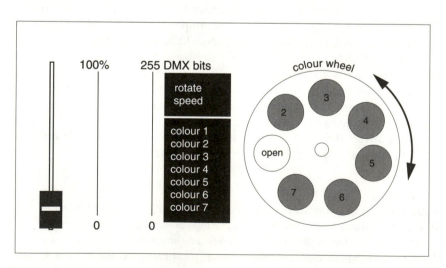

Figure 14.5 DMX control of a colour wheel

objects are being used in the optical train at the same time, and a lot of light is lost during the mixing process. Lighter pastels are easy and impressive, and with this type of colour system smooth fades from one colour to another are possible even if it may take some experimenting and a certain control of colour theory to reach the expected results. The colour mixing parameters should always be controlled as fading attributes. In some units they have to be set to 100% to provide light output (as in a Cyberlight, for example); inverting the colour mixing attributes in these cases means all colour mixing attributes can be at 0% when white light (no mix) is required.

Gobo attributes

Metal or glass projection masks are used both to project patterns near photographic images (in some cases) and to change the shape of the beam. They are usually mounted in a wheel similar to a colour wheel, which is rotated to place them in the path of the light beam. In addition to selecting a gobo, some units can rotate a gobo at variable speeds in both directions, both for effects or to fine tune positioning of the gobo for a projection. Gobo wheels are usually controlled by one stepping attribute, while another fading attribute is used for rotating (if rotation is possible).

Beam attributes

There are a lot of different parameters that can be used to control the beam, and some are called 'effects' even though these effects (like a prism) affect the beam. Generally, the parameters sorted under 'beam control' are iris, zoom, focus and shutters. All these parameters are controlled as 'fading' attributes as opposed to 'stepping'.

- *Iris*
The iris alters the size of the beam by masking it through the opening of a linear shutter.

- *Zoom*
A zoom is an optical lens system that is moved to provide a different projection angle for the beam. The beam size is altered and the amount of light being projected is distributed over the whole beam area, which means a smaller zoom angle will provide a brighter light.

- *Focus*
To be able to use projection masks like gobos it is necessary to be able to focus the beam for different projection distances. Also, the focus parameter

can be 'played' to provide 'morphing' effects fading from one pattern to another.

- *Shutters*

Some fixtures have motorized shutters (Martin PAL 1200, for example) functioning like shutters in a conventional profile lamp, providing remarkable beam control possibilities.

Effect attributes

Some fixtures provide a separate effect wheel with different prisms that can be used to project multiple images, filters for frost and diffusion or more colour correction filters. This wheel is controlled like a gobo wheel, as a fading or stepping parameter.

Moving light functions in consoles

The multitude of parameters involved in moving lights can make programming quite tedious and complex. While some products are better than others at simplifying the control of moving lights, there are a few functions most have in common.

There may be different solutions to how the control of moving light parameters is 'passed' from one playback to another, but each attribute can only be controlled from one playback at a time.

Masking

All moving light parameters except intensities are generally treated as LTP (lastest takes precedence) by a console. Masking is a powerful tool for changing how attributes are affected by different functions.

LTP attributes are either 'off', which means they are not controlled from any playback of the board at all and they will stay at the last position they were set to, or they are 'on' which means they are receiving a DMX value from 0 to 255. For example, if all attributes except colour (which is masked as 'off') are stored in a memory then this memory can be replayed without affecting the current colour of the fixture. Then a chase can be stored affecting only colour, and this chase can be replayed together with the other memory since they are 'speaking' to different attributes 'within' a fixture (see Fig. 4.4).

Moving lights in submasters

Submasters that handle both HTP dimmer intensities and LTP attributes can treat LTP channels in at least three ways. In addition to 'when' an attribute is passed on there may be masking (see above) allowing only 'certain' attributes to be affected (see also Chapter 4).

1. As soon as a submaster is moved attributes will jump to the control of that submaster.
2. As soon as a submaster is moved under a specified level (10%, for example) attributes will jump to the control of that master.
3. The submaster fader will control intensities as HTP and a key is pressed when attributes should jump to the control of that master. This way the control of attributes can be transferred from one playback to another without changing dimmer intensities.

Moving lights in cue playbacks

Usually attributes will be 'grabbed' by any cue that is started in a cue playback, regardless of whether or not they are controlled from a submaster. Some systems allow attributes to be masked so that a playback only 'steals' or affects certain attributes. This way a submaster may be controlling colour while positions are controlled by cues.

Focus presets

There are powerful tools for speeding up programming are memories that can be used as references in other memories, usually called focus presets. Imagine a focus preset consisting of all moving lights positioned to the centre of the stage. Every time a moving light is positioned to the centre of stage, that preset is recalled and stored as part of a 'larger' memory involving other lights and maybe other focus presets. This way there is a quick way of positioning any light to a predefined area.

When any 'larger' memory is recalled, all lights referring to the focus preset 'centre stage' will go to that position. If for some reason the 'centre stage' position is moved so that the lights are hitting the wrong area, only the focus preset 'centre stage' needs to be modified, and all 'larger' memories referring to 'centre stage' will automatically be updated. This way a lot of reprogramming can be done in a matter of minutes.

Palettes

Palettes are basically focus presets for parameters other than positions. There may be group palettes with preselected groups of fixtures (for example, all Cyberlights, every second Golden Scan, etc.), or colour palettes (for example, all fixtures and scrollers in red), or combined palettes (for example, all fixtures with open iris and white beam plus prism).

Home position

Some consoles allow the programming of a 'home position' for moving lights. Basically a home position is a memory setting all parameters so that a unit is directed, for example, to the 'centre of the stage with open iris, no effects and white light'. This is useful for quickly identifying a fixture, since setting all parameters to zero may set the light to no output and direct the beam straight up, where it can't be seen.

Fade times

Many systems allow a general fade time for fading LTP attributes and make all 'stepping' attributes change in the beginning of a fade, but some boards allow separate control of each parameter with wait and delay times from GO. This makes it possible to control almost every aspect of a transition, for example when the colour is changed, or to adjust the acceleration of the gobo rotation, etc.

Rigging moving lights

Follow the manufacturer's instructions when rigging, and make sure the unit is set to operate in a mode that is supported by the personality file in the control system. Test the unit by controlling each parameter directly as a DMX channel before converting them into attributes. This way you will get a better idea of what the unit is capable of and make sure all parameters function properly. Many problems with moving fixtures boil down to lack of termination of DMX in the last unit (see 'Analogue control and DMX512'), or the wrong operating mode/address being set before powering up.

Conclusion

The bottom line of controlling moving lights is that it is time consuming and brain rattling. Juggling multiple units with up to 30 control parameters in three-dimensional space with a fourth dimension of time involved just isn't easy, although control boards supporting moving light functions are getting good at compensating for this. Some consoles (Wholehog II, for example) have 'auto-generated effects' that can be used to create, for example, a circle movement with a variable diameter in no time at all. Another great aid is the graphics tablet, that allows all the functions of the fixtures to be mapped out and accessed by a digital pen on a drawing board. Some consoles (Avolites, for example) support a graphics tablet that allows CMY colour mixing directly on a colour diagram, plus positioning and following of actors from the same tablet by 'training' the fixtures to a two-dimensional (x/y) space representing the stage area. There are at least three systems (Autopilot (Wybron), Lighting Director (Martin) and Star Tracker (AVAB)) that monitor the three-dimensional space of the acting area through a transmitter, and send the control parameters directly from any stage position to a fixture through the control board.

Part 4 – Communication

Introduction

A live show production may involve equipment from different industries, such as lights, sound, projection and stage machinery. Since all this equipment is being used for the same result it would seem logical to have a single communications standard, so all control equipment could be connected with the same type of cable and connector and start communicating right away. One catch to this is that different kinds of data need to be communicated, and a standard meeting the requirements of all industries at the same time would require a very high data handling capacity, making it unreasonably expensive (if even possible) for most mid-sized and small venues. Instead, communication standards from different industries are used at the same time when equipment from different industries overlaps or interacts.

The following chapters provide a general understanding of where different communications standards used in the lighting industry come from and what they can be used for. An excellent book that provides a thorough explanation of each protocol is John Huntington (1994) *Control Systems for Live Entertainment*, Focal Press.

15 Communication standards (in the lighting industry)

A lighting console is a control device primarily designed to communicate with lighting equipment such as dimmers, scrollers and moving lights. To make this communication of control data possible there has to be a common 'language' with a specified 'grammar', and a standard for how this information is transported from one device to another (cables, connectors and electrical characteristics). This information is supplied in a specification of each communications standard.

Example
The main standard used from lighting consoles to dimmers and other lighting devices is called DMX512. If you are unfamiliar with DMX512 you may want to read Chapter 16 before this chapter.

Who defines a standard?

When there are several manufacturers of similar equipment, there will at first be different proprietary solutions to how each manufacturer's products communicate. This gets frustrating where the equipment from one manufacturer can't talk to the equipment of another, or requires extra 'translation' devices cluttering up the installation. A solution to this is for all manufacturers to unite around the same specification for communication. This is usually handled through a trade organization (see Appendix 1) where representatives of users and manufacturers cooperate to define and publish a standard specification that can be implemented throughout that section of the industry. Some manufacturers may still choose to continue using proprietary standards, because it meets the requirements of their systems in a better way than the official standard, or to support older product lines.

Example
Before DMX512 there were many different proprietary protocols for communication between lighting consoles and dimmers. DMX512 was specified by representatives of the industry through the United States Institute for Theater Technology (USITT).

Borrowed standards

Sometimes a standard from one industry is 'borrowed' and adapted to the requirements of another industry, which may lead to the original specification being revised and sub-specifications added.

Example
MIDI (Musical Instrument Digital Interface) was originally designed for the musical instrument industry to communicate notes played in one synthesizer to another. Now it is being used as a general protocol for communicating control data between show equipment like, for example, lighting consoles, video players, sound equipment, pyro effects and stage machinery. Sub-specifications of MIDI have been designed for this, such as MIDI Show Control and MIDI Machine Control.

What does a specification consist of?

The specification of a communication standard is a description of how fast a certain amount of data can be transported from one point to another. The speed is usually expressed as bps (bits per second) and the amount of data as the bandwidth.

Example
DMX512 can transmit up to 512 dimmer levels at a speed of 250 kbps with a maximum update rate for each level of 44.1 times per second (44.1 Hz).

Electrical and physical characteristics

There is also a part defining the electrical characteristics, and the physical cables and connectors recommended for transporting this data.

Example
A single DMX512 line can be transmitted over a distance of 1500 metres (5000 feet) in a shielded twisted pair cable of, for example, a Belden 9841 type. Up to 32 receiving devices (dimmers, for example) can be accommodated in one link. The transmitting device should have a 5-pin XLR female connector and the receiving device a male connector. The end device in each line should be terminated (see 'Analogue control and DMX512').

Open or closed loop

Some communication standards send information to receiving devices and never check if it was received properly. This is called an open loop or a unidirectional standard. Other standards are designed so information from the receiving devices can report back to the controlling device. This is called a closed loop or a bi-directional standard.

Example
DMX is an open loop standard, partly because this is less complicated to implement and more 'forgiving' in a show environment, where devices may be moved around and switched on or off without notice. Sometimes a separate data link is used to send dimmer monitoring information back to the lighting console to compensate for this.

Summary

The following are different communication standards you may run across in the lighting industry. The organization holding the specification of each standard is in brackets after the name of the standard (see Appendix 1).

From lighting consoles to lighting devices

Data from lighting consoles to dimmers or moving lights is a continuous stream with a lot of information constantly being updated in real time.

- *Analogue control 0–10 V (a* de facto *standard)*
This is often used in low-end equipment (see Chapter 16).

- *DMX512 (USITT)*
This is the main standard for dimmers and other lighting devices (see Chapter 16).

- *Ethernet (IEEE)*
This is a bidirectional standard for transmitting large amounts of data in general computer networks that are used in larger lighting installations to transmit DMX512 and other kinds of data. Implementations are proprietary to each manufacturer (see Chapter 17).

Although the above standards are the ones mainly used, it is also possible to come across one of the following:

- *AMX192 (USITT)*

This is an early analogue multiplex standard for communication to a total of 192 dimmers, nowadays mostly supported in Strand products. AMX192 may also be called CD80.

- *SMX (Strand)*

This was presented as an alternative to DMX and is mainly supported in Strand products.

- *D54 (Strand)*

This is an early multiplex standard for communication to a total of 384 dimmers mostly supported in Strand products to interface older equipment.

- *AVAB (AVAB)*

This is an early protocol for communication to a total of 256 dimmers prior to DMX, nowadays mostly supported in AVAB products to interface older equipment.

- *SDX (R.A. Gray Inc.)*

This is an alternative to DMX for communication to dimmers and other lighting devices, mostly supported in R.A. Gray Inc. show control products.

- *PMX (Pulsar)*

This is a proprietary moving lights protocol supported by Pulsar and Clay Paky products along with DMX512.

- *Lightwave Research (High End)*

This is a proprietary moving lights protocol supported by High End fixtures along with DMX512.

Between lighting consoles and other show equipment

Communication from one show controller to another usually consists of momentary commands to 'start a light cue' or 'rewind a tape', which are interpreted and executed by the receiving device immediately after they have arrived. This kind of data is usually called show control data (see Chapter 18).

Another way of trigging show control commands in a controller is to have a list of functions set up in the device that can be trigged by a contact closure, or just an incoming MIDI note or DMX512 level (see 'Macros'). Many lighting consoles support one or the other of these options, and some both.

- *MIDI (MMA)*

Many lighting consoles have proprietary implementations of musical MIDI commands that can trig board functions (See Chapter 18).

- *MIDI Show Control (MMA)*

Many lighting consoles have what is called a minimum recommended set of commands that are recognized (See Chapter 18).

- *MIDI Machine Control (MMA)*

So far, few (if any) lighting consoles are implementing MMC, which is mostly used for sound and stage machinery.

- *RS232, 485 (EIA)*

These are two of the most popular standard interfaces for serial communication in computers in general. Many lighting consoles have proprietary implementations so these ports can be used to receive or transmit show control information, or for connecting optional devices such as, for example, digitizers.

Synchronizing time-based events

When events need to be synchronized to a common time reference, this reference needs to be communicated to all involved devices. This is usually done through the MIDI port as MIDI Time Code or as SMPTE Time Code to an SMPTE port. The receiving devices will 'read' the time code and execute predefined commands from a list that is synchronized with the incoming time code.

Another solution is to let the time code be handled by a central Show Control device that sends show control data to the control devices involved at the appropriate times.

- *SMPTE Linear Time Code (SMPTE/ANSI)*

This is the 'original' time code which was developed for video and film editing, which is an audio signal (see 'MIDI and time code').

- *MIDI Time Code*

This is the 'MIDI version' of SMPTE Time Code, which can be used to send Time Code through the MIDI port of a lighting console (see 'MIDI and time code').

Show data between lighting consoles

There is a standard for transferring show data between lighting consoles and other lighting software such as off-line editors and plotting programs defined through the USITT. This is called Standard ASCII Light Cues. See 'ASCII Light Cues'.

16 Analogue control and DMX512

Today the most common standard for communication between a lighting console and lighting equipment such as dimmers, moving lights or scrollers is a digital serial protocol called DMX512. In low-end applications an earlier *de facto* standard in the form of analogue control is still being used. This chapter explains how they work, the differences between analogue and digital control and the advantages of each.

Analogue control

Early all-electric dimmers made it possible for a lighting console to communicate intensities by sending a very small DC current to the dimming circuit. This is called analogue communication. At first there was no standard for this communication, and as a result a dimmer could only be controlled by a lighting console designed to control that dimmer.

At some point most manufacturers started using the same control voltage; 0–10 volts. The dimmer compares the incoming voltage to a ramp for the output, 0 V = 0% out, 5 V = 50% out, 10 V = 100% out, etc. Today analogue control is still used in low-budget applications, club lighting and smaller theatre or concert equipment (Figure 16.1).

Advantages of analogue control

(a) The technology is simple and cheap to implement for manufacturers.
(b) It is easy to measure signals with simple equipment (voltmeter).
(c) Analogue control is a continuous signal with smooth, infinite resolution.
(d) Easy to adapt to other equipment such as relays, smoke machines, etc.

Limitations of analogue control

(a) Analogue control is parallel, which means it requires one physical lead per dimmer channel plus a common reference lead. This results in thick

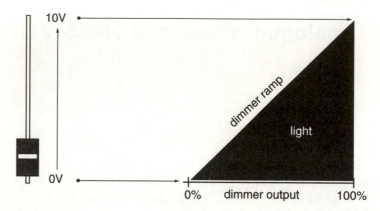

Figure 16.1 Analogue control of dimmer ramp

control cables, with large and expensive multi-pin connectors. The nature of these multi-pin connectors makes cable extensions complex.

(b)   Every lighting device has a unique physical link to the lighting console, which means equipment will usually be connected in a star configuration with the lighting console in the middle 'radiating' control cables to all devices (Figure 16.3).

(c)   Long control cables need to be buffered, because the control voltage will fall over large distances.

Multiplexing

An alternative to sending information in parallel with one dedicated control cable for each receiving dimmer is to multiplex the information. One form of multiplexing called 'time multiplexing' is, roughly speaking, a method of chopping up large amounts of simultaneous (parallel) information into small 'packets' and sending it quickly down a line to be interpreted at the other end. This is done so fast it 'seems' as if the whole packet arrived simultaneously. This kind of communication is called serial as opposed to parallel (Figure 16.2).

Advantages of multiplexing

- Information for hundreds of channels can be communicated in a single three- or four-lead cable, which simplifies handling, weight and cost of the control cables.

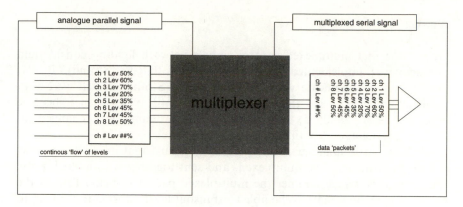

Figure 16.2 Multiplexing

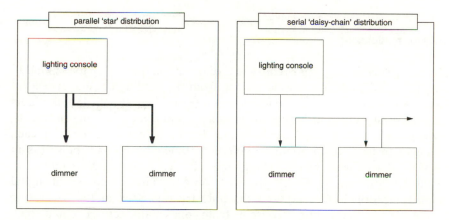

Figure 16.3 Parallel and serial signal distribution

- The star connection fundamental to parallel control isn't necessary, because the signal can be linked from device to device (see Figure 16.3). This simplifies rigging, since the lighting console can connect to the first dimmer, the first dimmer to the second, etc.

Limitations of multiplexing

- More sophisticated equipment and knowledge is required for measuring and analysing the control signal (see 'Troubleshooting DMX').
- A multiplexed signal cannot be split, merged or converted back to an analogue signal, without involving extra equipment (see Figure 16.5).

AMX192

One of the first multiplexed control signals between lighting console and dimmers was implemented in the 1980 Light Palette (Strand). It was designed to communicate with CD80 dimmers (Strand), which were very popular, and was called the CD80 protocol until 1986, when it became accepted as a standard by the USITT. The name was changed to AMX192 (Analogue Multiplexing for 192 channels).

AMX is partly analogue, which basically means that an analogue low-voltage control signal is multiplexed, and sent together with a clock pulse that 'identifies' which dimmer the multiplexed packet is meant for. At the time it was revolutionary to be able to transmit level information for up to 192 dimmers in a single, four-lead cable, but the partly analogue solution is pretty sensitive to ground loops and electrical 'noise' interference problems.

Digital multiplexing

In mid-1980s the trigging circuitry in a dimmer could be made to respond to digital signals, relating to exact values from the lighting console instead of 'differences in voltage to a reference point' (see Fig. 16.4). Manufacturers started designing and using proprietary digital multiplexing protocols, where each 'data packet' carried exact level information coded for each dimmer instead of an analogue reference timed by a clock pulse (as in AMX). There were several being marketed such as CMX (Colortran), K96 (Kliegl), and the AVAB protocol (AVAB). The advantages of digital communication were great, but the industry was back at the frustrating point where the lighting console from one manufacturer could only 'speak' to specific dimmers.

DMX512 – a revolution!

In 1986 representatives from major manufacturers in the lighting industry united at a USITT (see Appendix 1) conference and outlined this digital multiplexing lighting control standard. DMX512 has been a success which has truly revolutionized the lighting industry, allowing any lighting console following the standard to be connected to any lighting device capable of receiving it and working right away.

Parts of DMX are described in the examples in Chapter 15. These are some general aspects of DMX512. For more detailed information on how to make a proper DMX installation I can warmly recommend Adam Bennette's *Recommended Practice for DMX512, A Guide For Users and Installers*, USITT/PLASA.

DMX resolution

While an analogue signal has an 'infinite resolution' from 0 to 10 V, a digital signal has a 'definite resolution' with 8 'bits' for each DMX channel, which basically means 256 steps (0–255) from 0 to 100%. There is no specification for how the intermediate (between decimal values) steps are mapped from 0 to 100% since dimmer intensities are rarely plotted in smaller values. When DMX is used to control other lighting devices such as scrollers or moving lights the full resolution is often used, and referred to in handbooks for these devices. In these cases DMX values are usually written in decimal values (0–255) but sometimes they are also expressed in hexadecimal, which is a numerical system with a base of 16 that is expressed in combinations of letters (A–F) and numbers (0–9). There is plenty of literature which explains hexadecimal notation, so this will not be done here; instead I recommend getting a conversion table between decimal and hexadecimal.

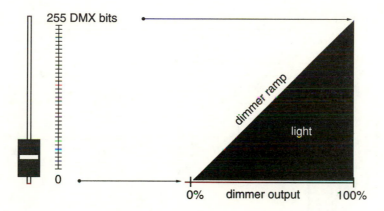

Figure 16.4 DMX256 bit dimmer ramp

DMX connector

The standard DMX connector is a 5-pin XLR, but only three pins are used for DMX. The two free pins are not defined by the standard, and basically they may be used for any proprietary data link as long as they comply electrically with the EIA (Electronics Industry Association) recommended standards for RS485, which is the EIA serial protocol that DMX512 is based on (see Appendix 1).

DMX pinout

Pin number	Function
1	Signal common (Shield)
2	Data−
3	Data+
4	No connection (Optional)
5	No connection (Optional)

DMX distribution

A single DMX512 line of up to 512 channels can be transmitted over a distance of 1500 metres (5000 feet) in a shielded twisted pair cable. Up to 32 receiving devices (dimmers, for example) can be accommodated in one link. The transmitting device should have a 5-pin XLR female connector and the receiving device a male connector. The end device in each line

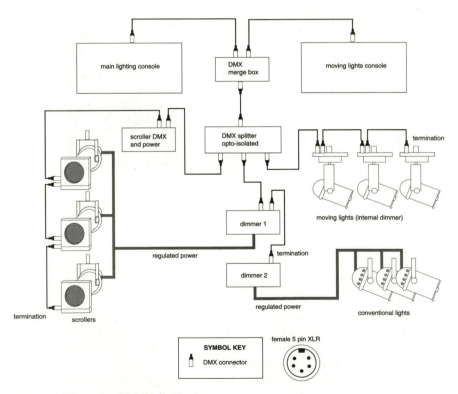

Figure 16.5 Example of DMX distribution

should be terminated. This protects the line from interference and is easily done with a resistor of approximately 120 ohms between "data+" and data− (pins 2 and 3). Some equipment does this automatically; if not, a DMX connector can be prepared as a terminator plug. If a DMX signal is split it should be buffered and opto-isolated before being redistributed into separate lines with individual termination to avoid, for example, high voltage caused by a malfunction in a dimmer returning to the console or the other lines. If several DMX signals are to be merged, a special merge box with a processor is required.

If more than 512 channels are required, several DMX lines can be used, but the internal numbering of each DMX line is always 1–512. If a line is used for DMX channels 513–1024, the output in the cable is still 1–512, and the instruments responding to the signals are still responding to 1–512. So, basically the lighting console might display these channels as 513–1024, but they are patched to outputs 1–512 in DMX line #2 (for example).

DMX is 'one way'

DMX is transmitted in one direction only, there is no return information to verify that the data has 'arrived' properly at its destination(s). Therefore a board may be transmitting correct DMX data to, for example, a dimmer rack, and a cable fault might stop the data from arriving, but there is no way for the dimmer to let the board 'know' this has happened, since there is no line 'back'. This kind of system is also called an 'open loop' and can be worked around with separate feedback lines or a separate return link (see 'Dimmer monitoring systems' in Chapter 12).

Troubleshooting DMX

One problem with serial data communication is troubleshooting. You can measure the Data +/− voltages in the control cable and make sure the line is intact, but it is not that easy to check the information being transmitted. Fortunately, there are dedicated instruments such as the Lil' DMXter (Goddard Design Co.) that are capable of both sending, receiving and analysing DMX data. These instruments allow you to check and even sample DMX data at different points in a DMX network.

Console DMX input

Some boards offer a facility for taking in an external DMX signal. This can be useful for different purposes:

- Running the show from another (guesting) console through the main system, using the house patch of the main system.
- Playing back cues from another board through the main board, so these can be stored as cues in the main system (see also 'ASCII Light Cues').
- Running effects or moving lights from an external board through the main board.
- Triggering macros or other functions in the main console.

After DMX512?

There are obvious restraints to DMX512 that prompt new solutions like Ethernet and networking (see Chapter 17), but it's a safe bet that DMX will be around for quite some time, just as analogue control continues to coexist with DMX. There are two main limitations of DMX:

- 512 channels in a single cable is no longer much, since moving lights and other equipment controlled from a console can consume several hundred channels. Being able to send more channels in a cable would simplify signal distribution.
- There is no defined feedback link, which is useful both for dimmer monitoring response and for other areas like intelligent positioning feedback from moving lights.

17   Ethernet and networking

When DMX512 was designed it was intended mainly for distributing light data to dimmers. Today it has become a control network for other DMX devices such as scrollers and moving lights. DMX was not intended for this, and recently another type of data network has been introduced to the lighting industry from the computer industry, allowing not only DMX, but all kinds of show data to be distributed in a high-performance network called Ethernet.

What is Ethernet?

Ethernet is a general specification by IEEE (Institute of Electrical and Electronic Engineers) that has been adopted in parts by lighting companies, and in some cases given proprietary names such as AVABNet (AVAB), ETCNet (ETC) or ShowNet (Strand). Until a standard for how show data is transported though Ethernet is designed and followed through, the industry will temporarily be back at the point of incompatibility prior to DMX. At the time of writing ESTA (Entertainment Services and Technology Association) are looking into this.

In an initial effort to standardize the use of Ethernet in the lighting industry, ESTA has produced a 'Recommended Practice for Ethernet Cabling Systems in Entertainment Lighting Applications'. This is an extract from that document that explains the basics of Ethernet:

Simply put, Ethernet is a communications network that operates at 10Mb/s (million bits per second), which is 40 times faster than DMX512. Ethernet is bi-directional; data may be sent and received from each connected unit (frequently called a node) on a network. There is no central controller in Ethernet. Each node 'listens' to the network and waits for a quiet moment. When it finds one, it begins sending data.

NOTE: There is a faster Ethernet standard, allowing 100 Mb/s of data to be transported, which is not being used in the lighting industry at the moment, but which may be implemented in the future.

What is networking?

Networking means interconnecting equipment with a mutual communications protocol. It is a technique used, for example, to interconnect office computers, so that all users can share the same printer. Networking can be applied to a lighting control system to solve intercommunication between different devices. The following are examples of lighting devices that can be interconnected in a show control network:

- lighting consoles, to provide multi-console operation
- backup systems, for full tracking
- designer's remote stations
- remote video interfaces
- dimmers, for lighting data and feedback monitoring
- moving lights, for control and feedback
- remote focus units.

The network 'transports' show data

Shown below are examples of show data that can be 'translated' into Ethernet and distributed around a performance area in an inexpensive cable, to be intercepted by other devices and translated back to its original form.

- DMX512 data
- video data
- show data
- MIDI data
- time code data (MTC or SMPTE)
- serial data (RS232 etc....).

Basic terms involved in networking

A network can be configured in a lot of different ways, but to make it work properly there are certain rules that have to be followed concerning cable lengths, types of cables and termination requirements of these cables, different topologies and the number of devices that can be involved in each segment of a network.

This is an introduction to the basic terms involved, not an installation guide. For information about how to design an Ethernet network, follow the guidelines from the manufacturer of the equipment you wish to network and the ESTA 'Recommended Practice for Ethernet Cabling Systems in Entertainment Lighting Applications'.

Networks and LANs

When equipment is interconnected so that data can be distributed, the result is called a network. A network within a restricted area (such as a theatre) is sometimes called a Local Area Network (LAN). A lighting console connected to a designer's remote station and a DMX distributor in a dimmer room is an example of a LAN.

Topologies and segments

Devices in a network can be physically interconnected in three basic ways called topologies. These topologies are linear, star, or ring. Topologies are like 'building blocks' that can be combined within the same network.

(a) A linear topology interconnects all devices on one segment, and can be made directly between two or more devices. The length of a segment and the amount of devices that it will support can be augmented by a repeater. A repeater counts as one of the devices on the network, and requires AC power. If one device goes down, the whole segment will go down. It is important that each device in the ends of a segment is terminated and that only one end is grounded (Figure 17.1).

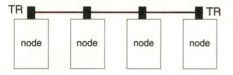

Figure 17.1 Linear topology

(b) A star topology links all devices to a central point at which a distribution device, called a concentrator or a HUB, is required to distribute information to the devices on each outgoing line, called a segment. If one device goes down the rest won't be affected, but if the central HUB goes down the whole network will go down (Figure 17.2).

(c) A ring topology links all devices together in a loop from one device to the next (etc.), which makes it suitable over long distances since data is repeated and amplified as it is passed around the ring. Ring topologies are not that common in show networks, because if one device goes

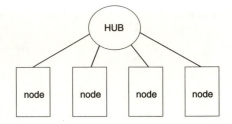

Figure 17.2 Star topology

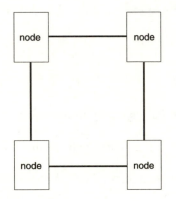

Figure 17.3 Ring topology

down, the whole network will go down, and no device can be added or removed without taking the whole network down (Figure 17.3).

Combined topologies

The topologies recommended by ESTA are linear bus, simple star, bussed backbone, and hierarchical star topology. The latter two are combinations of linear and star topologies. Basically topologies can be combined in a number of different ways as long as the rules for each cable type are respected, see 'A rule of thumb' at the end of this chapter (Figure 17.4).

Cable types

Four different kinds of cables are covered by the IEEE standard, each suitable for certain situations and requirements. Different cable types may be combined, even though it is recommended that only one type of extension cable is used within the installation.

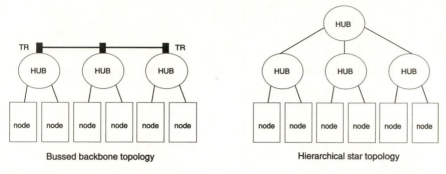

Bussed backbone topology   Hierarchical star topology

Figure 17.4 Combined topologies

(a) *Unshielded twisted pair (also called UTP or 10BASE-T)*
UTP is a good alternative both for long distances and fixed installations due to the relatively low cost of the cable, and the fact that it can be updated to future 100 Mb/s Ethernet (100BASE-T). It is basically a four-lead telecommunications cable that requires a central HUB, which means it can be used for star topologies only. The HUB is an active device that requires electrical power, if the HUB fails the network will be inoperative. Several HUBs can be connected with a linear backbone bus. There is a two-port passive HUB sometimes called a 'null concentrator' that can be used to connect two devices with a UTP cable (Figure 17.5).

- Maximum length of cable for a segment is 100 m (330′).
- Maximum two nodes per segment.
- Minimum length of cable between two nodes is 0.6 m (2′).
- Cable specification: 10BASE-T (10 means 10 Mb/s, BASEband, T stands for UTP).
- The connector used is a telecommunications standard RJ45 8-pin connector.

Pin number	Function	PDS/258A wire colour
1	Transmit+	T2 white–orange stripe
2	Transmit−	R2 white–orange stripe
3	Receive+	T3 white–green stripe
6	Receive−	R3 green–white stripe

(b) *Thin Net (10BASE-2)*
ThinNet uses a 50 ohm coaxial cable with BNC connectors, and is suited for linear topologies and large systems with many nodes and a star topology. The cables and connectors are fairly rugged but should be handled with care. Each segment has to be terminated with a 50 ohm BNC terminator;

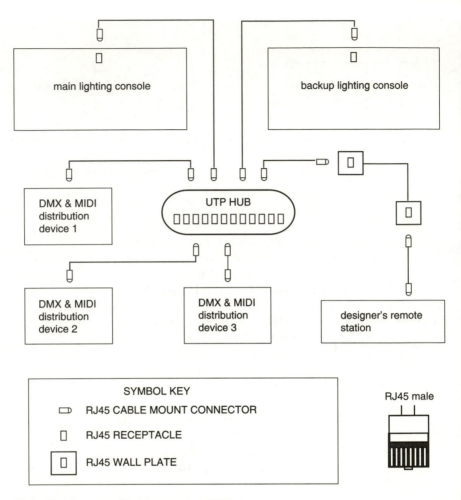

Figure 17.5 Example of multiple segment UTP

if the terminator is removed that segment will cease to function. A ThinNet HUB is used to create a star topology. Several HUBs can be connected with a linear backbone bus. ThinNet will probably not support future use of 100 Mb/s Ethernet (Figure 17.6).

- Maximum length of cable for a segment is 185 m (607').
- Maximum 30 nodes per segment.
- Minimum length of cable between two nodes is 0.5 m (1.5').
- Cable specification: 10BASE-2 (10 means 10 Mb/s, BASEband, 2 stands for 200 m).
- The connector used is a 50 ohm BNC connector, with isolated ground.

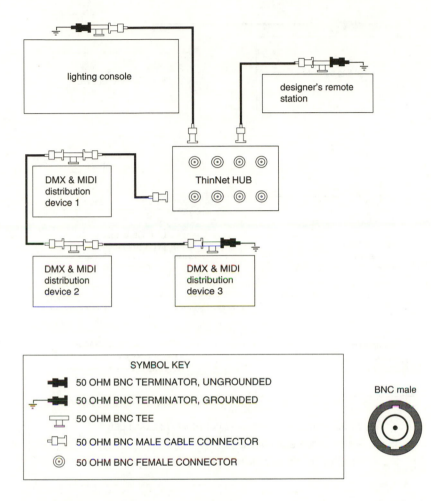

Figure 17.6 Example of multiple segment ThinNet

(c) *Optical fibre (10BASE-FL)*

Data can be transformed into light impulses that are immune to electrical noise. These light impulses are transported in an optical fibre which has a very high data handling capacity over long distances, a segment can be up to 1 km (0.6 miles) long. On the other hand fibre is expensive, requires careful handling and protection of cables and does not allow additional nodes on a segment, which makes it most suitable as a long-distance backbone for HUBs in a ThinNet or UTP network (Figure 17.7).

- Maximum length of cable for a segment is 1000 m (0.6 miles).
- Maximum two nodes per segment.

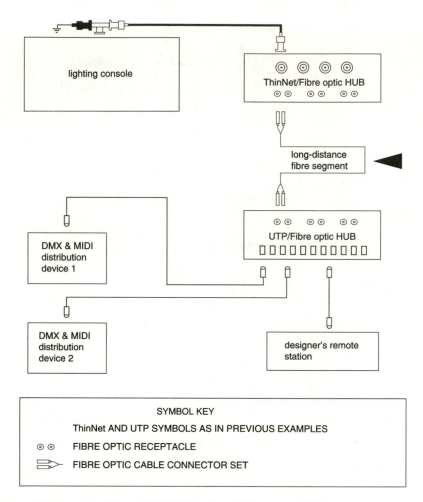

Figure 17.7 Example of fibre with ThinNet and multiple segment UTP

- No minimum length of cable between two nodes.
- Cable specification: 10BASE-FL (10 means 10 Mb/s, BASEband, FL stands for fibre).
- Connectors require special tools and expertise.

(d) *ThickNet (10BASE-5)*

ESTA does not recommend ThickNet. If long distances are an important feature, ThinNet with repeaters or optical fibre is probably more economical.

Repeaters

When a segment needs to be prolonged over the specified maximum cable length, or when more devices than specified need to be incorporated, a repeater is used. A repeater counts as one of the devices on the network, and requires AC power.

A rule of thumb

Always follow the instructions of each manufacturer and the guidelines in the ESTA 'Recommended Practice for Ethernet Cabling Systems in Entertainment Lighting Applications'. There is a rule of a thumb that an Ethernet network may be configured in any way following the guidelines above, as long as the 5–4–3 rule can be applied between any two nodes:

- no more than five segments in series
- no more than four HUBs
- no more than three populated segments.

18 MIDI and time code

MIDI (Musical Instrument Digital Interface) was developed in the early 1980s as an interface between synthesizers from different manufacturers. Basically it was designed so that one keyboard can play sounds in several other keyboards by communicating the notes that are played and how hard they are hit. This information can be sent in 16 different 'layers' called MIDI channels. Every receiving keyboard can listen to channel messages on one or more of these channels. Certain messages can be sent to all devices, regardless of channel. These are called system messages.

Basic MIDI glossary

Most of the 'language' of MIDI comes from the music industry. The following is a basic glossary of some terms that are useful to know:

- *MIDI channels*
There are 16 MIDI channels, and every channel can have channel messages such as notes, velocity, controllers or program change.

- *Omni*
When a device receives or transmits on all of the 16 channels, it is in omni mode.

- *Note*
Each MIDI channel can transmit 0–127 notes as NOTE_ON and NOTE_OFF commands with an intensity indicating how hard they were played (see 'Velocity'). Middle C on a keyboard corresponds to note 60. Notes are usually used to transmit function keys in non-standard lighting console implementations. Notes are channel messages.

- *Velocity*
How hard or loud a key was played is translated into the velocity of that note in values from 0 to 127. An 'average' velocity is 64. Velocity is some-

times used to transmit intensities in non-standard lighting console implementations. Velocity values are channel messages.

● *Controllers*
These are messages for any type of continuous fader values, such as volume
or pitch bend. There can be 0–120 controllers with values from 0 to 127.
Controllers are sometimes used to send fader values in non-standard lighting console implementations. Controllers are channel messages.

● *Program change*
This is a message used to change sound programs in slave keyboards from
the master keyboard. There can be 0–127 program change messages.
Program change is sometimes used to activate cues in non-standard lighting
console implementations. Program change is a channel message.

● *System exclusive*
There are messages that can be sent to all channels in a system, these are
called system messages. System exclusive messages are used to allow manu-
facturers to send any kind of product-specific message in a MIDI format.
This is a commonly used MIDI message in lighting console applications of
MIDI.

● *Tempo*
The tempo of a song is a musical reference to how fast the song is played.
MIDI has a timing clock that is sent out with song position pointers. This is
not the same as MIDI Time Code (see 'SMPTE and MIDI Time Code').

● *MIDI sequencer*
A sequencer is like a recorder that can store and replay MIDI messages in
real time. This is used like a multi-track recorder, except that only the MIDI
'notes' being played are stored, not the actual sounds. The MIDI data is
played back through a synthesizer(s) to recreate the song (Figure 18.2).

The physical side of MIDI

The MIDI specification is held by the IMA (International MIDI
Association, see Appendix 1). Put simply, MIDI is a communications net-
work designed to connect low-cost synthesizers. MIDI is unidirectional; a
device can receive MIDI through a MIDI In port, transmit through a MIDI
Out port and send an opto-isolated copy of the MIDI In port to a MIDI
Thru connector so that several devices can be daisy-chained. Usually a
MIDI configuration is of a master–slave type, with one device controlling
several others. All connectors are 180° five-pin DIN female connectors, and

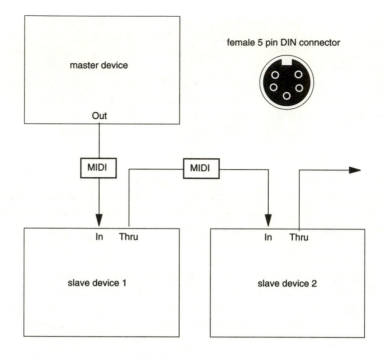

Figure 18.1 Example of a standard MIDI setup

all cables use standard, shielded twisted pair wires and male connectors. Cable lengths should normally not exceed 50 feet, but there are devices that can send MIDI over very long distances (Figure 18.1).

MIDI in lighting consoles

MIDI was pretty simple to understand, cheap to implement and, above all, it was an official standard. Therefore MIDI started getting implemented in all kinds of sound equipment, such as reverbs and mixers. MIDI was adopted in parts by lighting manufacturers too, and the music interface was being used for a lot of different things that were never intended from the start. 'Notes' and 'volume' data was being used in a completely non-standard way to trig lighting functions and things were pretty confused for a while (and they still are in some cases). Even though it takes an understanding of musical terms, MIDI and lighting consoles to use these non-standard applications there is a good side too, because it usually allows any keyboard with a MIDI Out to trig simple functions in a lighting console with a MIDI In. The following are some common non-standard applications of MIDI in lighting consoles.

● *'Playing' console functions through MIDI*
Some lighting consoles implement MIDI so that the lighting console can be controlled from, for example, a MIDI keyboard, responding with light channels to notes and intensities to show how hard the notes were played (MIDI velocity).

● *Lighting console to lighting console to extend a system*
MIDI is sometimes used to link two boards together, so both can be operated from the control panel of one, providing an extended system. Basically, faders and function keys are sent as, for example, MIDI 'notes' and 'controllers' from one board to the other, and the second board is set up to control additional lighting devices.

● *Tracking backup*
Two boards may be linked so that the main console sends all keys and faders as MIDI to a backup console that tracks through the show, ready to take over if the main system should break down.

● *Recording board functions in real time*
Faders and function keys can be sent as, for example, MIDI 'notes' and 'controllers' from the lighting console and recorded in real time in a MIDI

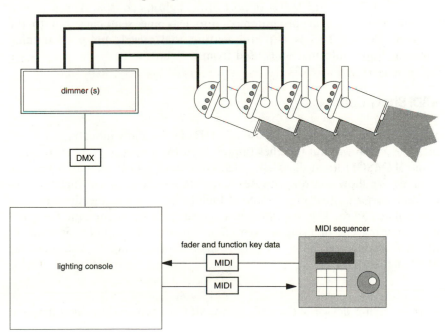

Figure 18.2 Example of lighting console and MIDI sequencer

'recorder' called a sequencer. Afterwards this data can be played back in real time through the MIDI In port of the board and 'play' the board as a 'ghost operator'. A sequencer can be synchronized with other equipment too, to create automated shows (see SMPTE and MIDI Time Code on p. 182).

● *MIDI clock trigging effects*
Some boards can 'listen' to the timing clock of MIDI, which is based on the tempo of the MIDI 'song' being played. This clock can be used to control the tempo of an effect. To edit the speed of the effect, the whole tempo of the 'song' has to be remapped, so in situations where this is vital (as in show control) SMPTE Time Code or MIDI Time Code is used instead (see SMPTE and MIDI Time Code on p. 182).

● *Data to dimmers*
In a few cases MIDI has been implemented to communicate directly with dimmers, which basically isn't a very good idea because the bandwidth (data handling capacity) of MIDI was never designed for this kind of information. Although this may work in very small installations it is highly recommended to use a small lighting console with a MIDI interface instead.

● *Capturing MIDI data*
Some lighting consoles have the capacity to 'capture' a MIDI command string that is sent to the MIDI In port of the lighting console. This captured command can then be programmed into lists and sent back out to the receiving device. This is a useful feature that speeds up programming since the 'right' information is used from the start.

MIDI Show Control

In an effort to standardize the use of MIDI in the show industry, a theatre message group was put together though the MMA to specify a MIDI Show Control (MSC) format. Basically, MSC specifies a set of commands that are reserved for show control purposes and puts show equipment into the general categories of Lighting, Sound, Machinery, Video, Projection, Process Control and Pyro. This way there is a specific standard command for starting a lighting cue or firing a pyro effect, instead of a million proprietary implementations of 'notes' and other commands being sent around the MIDI network.

● *Device IDs*
Each receiving device has an ID in an MSC situation. Messages are sent from a controlling device to a receiving device that checks this ID and the category (= command format, such as 'lighting', for example). If these are

not right, the command is ignored, which is a safety measure. Therefore this ID has to be set up in the lighting console (unless it is a fixed ID, check in the lighting console manual). There is also a global 'all call' command that MSC devices may respond to.

● *Recommended minimum set*
MSC does not specify which commands or data should be implemented in a device. Basically this means that a product that is 'MSC compatible' may possibly only recognize two or three commands. There are three 'recommended minimum sets' of general commands, and most lighting console manufacturers implement the absolute minimum set consisting of three commands:

GO: Starts next cue, or a specified cue number.
STOP: Stops cues in progress.
RESUME: Resumes cues in progress that have been stopped.

Besides this some also include the following commands:

FIRE: Triggers a macro in the board.
ALL_OFF: Turns off all outputs without changing settings (blackout).
RESTORE: Restores outputs after an ALL_OFF (undo blackout).
RESET: Stops all actions and initializes a state equivalent to a newly powered-up condition and loads the top of the show to standby.

These are summarized explanations and only a few of the most common commands that are implemented. For a more extensive specification of each command, get the full specification from the IMA (see Appendix 1).

● *Safety*
A receiving device will respond to an MSC command provided all local safety devices are in control and applied. MSC in no way replaces any aspect of normal performance safety, which is stated clearly in the specification.

MIDI Machine Control (MMC)

MMC was designed to standardize how MIDI should be implemented to control time-based and transport-oriented equipment such as, for example, audio and video tape decks. The MMC specification is extensive and not implemented much in lighting consoles, and therefore it is not explained further here. To get more information about MMC contact the IMA for the full specification or see the bibliography at the end of this book.

SMPTE and MIDI Time Code

Basically time code is just a way of sending 'time' coded as a data stream, through, for example, an audio cable or a MIDI cable so that several devices can share the same time reference. Time Code originated in the video business, where it was used to synchronize multiple video players for editing purposes. Therefore the smallest component of a time code is a video frame, which can be 25–30 frames/second depending on different standards. The format for Time Code is hours/minutes/seconds/video frames, and the specification for Time Code is held by the Society of Motion Picture and Television Engineers (SMPTE). Since Time Code is an audio signal, it is sometimes converted to MIDI as MIDI Time Code so it can be sent digitally to devices that only have a MIDI port.

Some lighting consoles are capable of receiving and/or transmitting Time Code and executing a list of commands that are set to different 'times'. This is a great way of synchronizing lighting equipment with other equipment in 'canned' or 'timebased' parts of a show.

19 ASCII Light Cues

The information that is stored as a show in a lighting console can be reloaded into the same brand and model, but is usually not compatible with any other lighting console. This means that if you are setting up the same show with a different console, or replacing a console with another type of console, you will have two options:

- If the new console has a DMX in option, it may be possible to 'capture' the output from the old console and store as cues in the new console. All other information like fade times, cue texts, patch or effects will have to be reprogrammed.
- Reprogram the whole show from scratch.

A standard show format

There is a standard defined by USITT for storing and reading light cues as an ASCII text file (ASCII stands for American Standard Code for Information Interchange and is a standard for text files). This standard makes it possible to transfer show data between the following:

- different lighting consoles compatible with ASCII Light Cues
- lighting consoles and standard word processors
- lighting consoles and spreadsheets/databases (for example Excel)
- lighting consoles and lighting software like off-line editors or plotting programs compatible with ASCII Light Cues.

Editing an ASCII Light Cues file

The standard is defined for most basic parts of a show such as groups, cues, times, patch and texts. Proprietary functions like effects or moving lights information can be tagged as manufacturer specific and transfer between consoles of the same type.

An ASCII file can be created as a text file in a word processor and loaded into a console, or exported from a console into a word processor (for example). A file shall always have:

1. A heading (Beginning of Data Stream).
2. Show data (cues, groups, submasters . . .).
3. An ending (End of Data Stream).

This is an example of a short file from an AVAB Presto console with only two cues:

MANUFACTURER AVAB
CONSOLE PRESTO
IDENT 3:0
CLEAR ALL

! After an exclamation mark like this, anything can be written. This
! information will be ignored when the file is loaded to a console.

! Cues

CUE 1.0
DOWN 1.0
UP 2.0
CHAN 1/65

CUE 2.0
DOWN 2.3
UP 3.0 2
CHAN 1/70 2/70 3/70 4/70 5/70 6/70

ENDDATA

1. *A heading (Beginning of Data Stream)*
An ASCII Light Cues file has to be started with information about the manufacturer, console model and the version of ASCII Light Cues being used to process the data. Also there is a CLEAR command that will clear all or part of a console memory when the file is loaded. CLEAR can be used to permit loading only the patch or separate cues from an ASCII file.

Keyword	Function
CLEAR	< clears all show data in the console
	Ex: ALL, SUBMASTERS, PATCH, CUES, GROUPS

CONSOLE   < identifies which console the show is from
                        Ex: EXPERT, PALT2, ACCSPRO

IDENT   < the ASCII Light Cues version being used
                        Ex: Currently 3.0

MANUFACTURER < the manufacturer's name
                        Ex: STRAND, COLORTRAN, AVAB, ETC

PATCH   < if a new patch is to be loaded (starts with a
                        1 before first channel)
                        Ex: PATCH 1 1< 40@100 = dimmer 40 to ch 1
                        at 100%

SET   < set parameters (dimmers or channels etc.)
                        Ex: CHANNELS ###, DIMMERS ###, PATCH
                        DEFAULT

$M-SPECIFIC   < manufacturer specific data
                        Ex: $ATTRIBUTES, $MIDI

Example of the beginning of an ASCII file:

MANUFACTURER STRAND   < Strand Lighting built this console
IDENT 3:0   < ASCII LC version 3.0 is being
                          followed
CONSOLE LIGHTPALETTE   < this is from a Light Palette console
CLEAR ALL   < all is cleared and replaced with this
                          file

PATCH 1 1<1@100 2<45@80   < dimmer 1 to channel 1 at 100%
                          < dimmer 45 to channel 2 at 80%

SET CHANNELS 300   < 300 channels
SET DIMMERS 512   < 512 dimmers

2. *Show data*

Show data is divided into three specified primary objects: CUES, GROUPS
and SUBMASTERS. Each of these can have attributes such as channels,
levels, times, etc.

Levels can be written as either decimal 0–100% or hexadecimal, which
allows defining levels to the full 256 steps of DMX512. Hexadecimal is a
numbering system with a base of 16 that is expressed with two or four
hexadecimal digits (0–9 and A–F) that may be preceded by an H. For

example, 90% = HE6. There are conversion tables for this in the ASCII Light Cues Specification from USITT.

Times are written from hours down to tenths of a second separated by colons and a decimal point: hour:minute:second:tenths.

Show data, primary objects:

CUE   < cue number
               Ex: 0 or 0.2 or 10 or 101.6 or 999.9

GROUP   < a group number
               Ex: 0 or 0.2 or 10 or 101.6 or 999.9

SUB   < submaster number, page number first if used
               Ex: SUB 1 or SUB 1 22 (page 1 sub 22)

Attributes of the primary keywords (cues, groups, submasters):

TEXT   < text
               Ex: GOING TO CATHYS 1ST DANCE

UP   < up time of this cue, delay after a comma
               Ex: 30, 2 (up 30, delay 2)

DOWN   < down time of this cue, delay after a comma
               Ex: 5, 4 (down 5, delay 4)

CHAN   < channels and levels of this cue, group or submaster
               Ex: 20@50 16@100 101@23

FOLLOWON   < follow-on time of next cue (cues only)
               Ex: 3 (3 seconds)

LINK   < link from this cue to another cue (cues only)
               Ex: 10 (cue 10)

PART   < eventual parts of this cue (cues and groups only)
               Ex: 1 (part 1)

$$M-SPECIFIC   < manufacturer specific cue, group or submaster data
               Ex: $$Profile

Example of Cue 1 Up 6 s, Down 3 s, Delay down 4 s, channels 1–3 at 50%:

CUE 1
TEXT Sunset cue opening ACT 5
DOWN 3,4
UP 6
CHAN 1@50 2@50 3@50 12@75 10@55 102@40

Example of Group 20.5:

GROUP 20.5
TEXT Red backlights drummer
CHAN 10@60 12@70 3@50 33@40

Example of sub 24 page 2, Up 6 s, Down 4 s:

SUB 2 24
TEXT Curtain lights
UP 6
DOWN 4
CHAN 90@70 92@70

Example of a cue with a manufacturer-specific colour attribute:
CUE 1.0
DOWN 3.0
UP 2.0
CHAN 1/65
$$COLOR 1/1

3. *An ending (End of Data Stream)*
The end of an ASCII Light Cues file is marked by the keyword ENDDATA.
    A complete description is available from USITT in the publication *ASCII Text Representation for Lighting Console Data*. This can be ordered from the USITT (see Appendix 1).

20   Troubleshooting

With a lighting console there are four problem areas:

1. operator errors
2. bugs in the software
3. faulty power
4. faulty DMX installation.

1. Operator errors

Whether due to incomplete manuals or the fact that switching from one type of system to another can be confusing, operator errors are common. The error can be a simple misunderstanding of how the system works or the fact that the system cannot do what was expected. The only solutions to this are accurate handbooks and customer phone support service from the manufacturer.

2. Bugs in the software

Sometimes a series of commands can make a console 'confused' resulting in a 'freeze'. If the console 'freezes' at the same point every time that command(s) is entered, there is probably a bug in the software; if it does not, it is probably something else. When a bug causes a 'freeze', all information that has been input up to that point may be lost (which can be a small disaster). Therefore shows should be saved at regular intervals. You cannot 'fix' a bug, but you may be able to work your way around it once you have isolated what causes it. Nowadays most systems are thoroughly debugged, but bugs may still occur; a good customer phone support service from the manufacturer can help to deal with this.

3. Faulty power

Lighting consoles and other computerized systems can be sensitive about their power feed. Unstable power, electrical noise, dips and spikes are hard to measure and may cause the lighting console to 'halt', reboot, or corrupt a memory that will halt the lighting console when a certain cue is played back. If faulty power is suspected the easiest solution is to use a high-quality Uninterruptible Power Supply (UPS) that will filter out these impurities from the power feed to the lighting console.

- A power generator is an unstable power source, which can fluctuate outside the limits accepted by the circuitry inside the lighting console.
- Noise on the power feed is generated by any equipment with a rapidly switching on/off cycle such as, for example, a dimmer, fluorescent lights, or a welder.
- Spikes and dips are temporary surges on the power feed that can be initiated, for example, by a central AC being turned on or off.
- If a corrupt show is suspected:
  (a) Make sure you have saved your show to a disk.
  (b) Reset the lighting console, reload the show and try playback again; if it freezes again there may be corrupt information in the show.
  (c) Try loading the same show in another system, if the same fault appears, it is most definitely a corrupt show (provided you have not entered a command which is a bug in the software, which will cause a stop when played back in any system).

NOTE: A way of 'cleaning up' a corrupt show is to make a transfer to an ASCII Light Cue file (if possible), where all information is displayed in text format and any 'corrupt' information is easily spotted and corrected. Then load the show back into the lighting console.

4. Faulty DMX installation

The DMX wiring is a lifeline that runs through the whole system, and a faulty DMX installation may send electrical noise or voltage straight into the heart of your lighting console due to lack of opto-isolation, or cause all kinds of problems with flickering or floating lights due to lack of termination or bad ground wiring. All these problems can be avoided by following the *Recommended Practice for DMX512* guidelines (by Adam Bennette, a PLASA/USITT publication).

Appendix 1 – Contact information

This appendix provides contact information for lighting industry associations, organisations holding standards used in the lighting industry and manufacturers discussed in this book.

1. Lighting industry organizations

ESTA (Entertainment Services and Technology Association)
875 Sixth Avenue, Suite 2302, New York, NY 10001
Tel: +1 212 244 1505, Fax: +1 212 244 1502
Email: info@esta.org   WWW:http//www.esta.org/

ESTA is a trade association representing the North American entertainment technology industry, dedicated to promoting professionalism and growth in the industry. ESTA has a Technical Standards Program which creates standards and recommended practices for the industry in a variety of areas including Control Protocols, Truss and Rigging, and Fog and Smoke. ESTA's Member Directory is available in print and on-line at ESTA's website.

PLASA (Professional Lighting and Sound Association)
7 Highlight House, St Leonards Road
Eastbourne BN21 3UH, England.
Tel: +44 (0) 1323 410335, Fax: +44 (0) 1323 646905
WWW:http//www.plasa.org.uk/plasa/

PLASA is the UK-based entertainment technology trade association which presents the international Light & Sound Show every September in London. Its publishing activities include two magazines – *Lighting + Sound International* and *Sound + Communication Systems International*. They publish a yearbook and a full listing of all members on the Internet. The association also provides a comprehensive range of technical standards, and industry-specific and business services for its members.

VPLT (Professional Lighting and Sound Association of Germany)
Vahrenwalder Str. 205–207
D30165 Hannover, Germany
Tel: +49 (0) 511 373 02 77, Fax: +49 (0) 511 373 04 23
WWW:http://www.pavilion.co.uk/plasa/vplt

The association of the leading manufacturers, distributors and suppliers in
Germany. Individual memberships have been available since 1995. VPLT
helps establish contacts for people who want to import from, or export to,
Germany. The association's work includes the areas of standards, publica-
tions, education, and government and international cooperation.

USITT (United States Institute for Theater Technology)
8–10 West 19th Street, Suite 5A
New York, NY 10011
Tel: +1 315 463 6463
WWW.http//www.ffa.ucalgary.ca.usitt/

Non-profit membership association comprised of individuals, organizations,
manufacturers and suppliers specializing in all aspects of technical production and design in the performing arts industry. USITT produces an Annual
Conference & Stage Expo, publishes *TD & T* and *Sightlines*, sponsors projects, programmes, research, symposia and exhibits and develops industry
standards for safe, efficient and ethical practices.

2. Organizations holding standards used in the lighting industry

EIA (Electronic Industries Association)
2001 Pennsylvania Ave, N.W.
Washington, DC 20006
Tel: +1 202 457 4966

Publishes the EIA Recommended Standards for serial communication such
as RS232, 485, etc.

IMA (International MIDI Association)
23634 Emelita Street
Woodland Hills, CA 91367
Tel: +1 818 598 0088

Publishes and holds all MIDI standards, including MIDI, MSC, MMC and
MTC.

SMPTE (Society of Motion Picture and Television Engineers)
595 West Hartsdale Avenue
White Plains, NY 10607, USA
Tel: +1 914 761 1100

Publishes the SMPTE Time Code standards and some others.

3. Manufacturers discussed in this book

ADB
Leuvensesteenweg 585,
B-1930 Zaventem, Belgium
Tel: +32 (2) 722 17 11, Fax: +32 (2) 722 17 64

AVAB
Samsmästaregatan 32B
S-422 62 Hisings Backa, Sweden
Tel: +46 (0) 31 58 52 00, Fax: +46 (0) 31 58 29 99
www.avab.se

Avolites
184 Park Avenue
Park Royal, London NW10 7XL, England
Tel: +44 (0) 181 965 8522, Fax: +44 (0) 181 965 0290
www.avolites.demon.co.uk

Celco
Hawley Mill, Hawley Road, Dartford
Kent DA2 7SY, England
Tel: +44 (0) 1322 282218, Fax: +44 (0) 1322 282292
www.celco.co.uk

Compulite
3, Haroshet St. New In, Zone
Ramat-Hasharon, 47279, Israel
Tel: +972 (3) 540 1268, Fax: +972 (3) 540 1276
www.compulite.com

ETC North America
3030 Laura Lane
Middleton, WI 53562, USA
Tel: +1 608 831 4116, Fax: +1 608 836 1736
Toll free number (in the US): 1 800 688 4116
www.etcconnect.com

EDI
1675 NW 216th Avenue
Hillsboro, OR 97124, USA
Tel: +1 503 645 5533, Fax: +1 503 629 9877
Toll free number (in the US): 1 800 547 2690

High End
2217 West Braker Lane
Austin, TX 78758, USA
Tel: +1 512 836 2242, Fax: +1 512 837 5290
www.highend.com

Strand Lighting
Grant Way, Isleworth
Middlesex TW7 5QD, England
Tel: +44 (0) 181 560 3171, Fax: +44 (0) 181 568 2103
www.strandlight.com

Transtechnik
Ohmstr. 1–3,
D-83607 Holzkirchen, Germany
Tel: +49 8024 990 0, Fax: +49 8024 990 300

Flying Pig Systems
53 Northfield Road
London W13 9SY, England
Tel: +44 (0) 181 579 5665, Fax: +44 (0) 181 579 8469
www.flyingpig.com

Zero 88 Lighting Ltd
Usk House. Llantarnam Park
Cwmbran NP44 3HD, England
Tel: +44 (0) 1633 838088, Fax: +44 (0) 1633 867880

Appendix 2 – An historical overview of some manufacturers

Part of the background research for this book consisted of looking into the history of some of the main manufacturers of lighting consoles. The material here gives a timeline for how different consoles have evolved, together with a little about the philosophy of each company. There are and have been more manufacturers but these are the most prominent ones at the time of writing this book. There is contact information in Appendix 1 and the trade associations listed there can provide up-to-date information on other manufacturers.

Besides the 'US market: a general background', each section is a company profile with release dates and some information on the main lighting consoles of that company. The companies are listed in alphabetical order.

ADB (Belgium)

In 1920 Adrian De Backer founded this company and started manufacturing electrical equipment used by laboratories.

- 1922 His first client in lighting control was Professor Picard from the University of Bruxelles who ordered nine rheostat dimmers. Around 1925 ADB developed this into a product line for lighting control in theatres, music halls and movie theatres. Tracking wire control systems were added to control the rheostat dimmers and various large installations were made around the world.
- 1960 The first memory system was produced, the FIM, which stands for Ferrite (core) Instant Memory. It was a two-scene preset board with memory group fading, and one of the first boards was installed at the National Opera in Bruxelles.
- 1972 The first Memolight memory system utilizing a tape recorder instead of a ferrite core as random access memory storage was presented, with channel faders for setting up lights and a channel keypad facility. Two years later a new version of the Memolight was released using a floppy disk instead of tape for memory retrieval. This system could han-

dle up to 360 channels and was popular all over the world. One was still in use in 1996 at the Teatro Colon of Buenos Aires.

- 1974 ADB came out with the Memo 48, a 48-channel memory console for smaller venues that had an optional one-scene or two-scene channel fader panel for plotting cues manually. Also Masterlight, a 120-channel version, was released.
- 1980 ADB presented the Megalight which replaced the Memolight, and had a capacity for 360 channels.
- 1983 The first memory console to use a mouse for setting channel levels was released. The 120-channel S20 replaced the Masterlight and would later be replaced by the Tenor. A larger version called S28 replaced the Megalight and had a capacity for 1024 channels.
- 1994 The Vision was presented, a 2048-channel state-of-the-art theatre console with integrated software for accommodating moving lights and colour scrollers.

ARRI (discontinued)

An English company manufacturing lighting equipment for the film industry. In 1985 they started a theatre controls division to compete with Strand by having a full product line including dimmers, lighting fixtures and boards. A distribution agreement was signed with ETC to distribute rebadged ETC boards in Europe which had been done before by TBA. Even though the boards were pretty successful, ARRI (GB) decided not to renew the agreement in 1995 and the theatre division was closed down.

- 1984 ETC Idea had been rebadged for TBA as the TBA Image.
- 1985 ETC Concept 250 had been rebadged for TBA as the TBA Imagination.
- 1985 The ETC Vision was rebadged as the ARRI Image.
- 1987 The ETC Expression was rebadged as the ARRI Imagine 250.
- 1987 The ETC Concept was rebadged as the ARRI Imagine 500.
- 1991 The ETC Microvision was rebadged as the ARRI Mirage.
- 1993 The ETC Expression 2 was rebadged as the ARRI Imagine 3.

AVAB (Sweden)

In 1971 engineers Torsten Palm and Sture Rönnbäck founded AVAB in Gothenburg, Sweden. They made psychedelic light organs, analogue touring dimmers and a 16-channel, six group manual preset board in a small Antler briefcase to go along with it. Despite sales going well they couldn't cash a sales commission owing to Kent Flood, a theatre director, lighting designer and technician and his colleague Ralph Dahlberg, so they offered shares in the company instead and the quartet set out to manufacture theatre controls.

- 1976 AVAB presented a three-scene preset board with three group switches for each channel in each scene and the first dipless crossfade solution in a manual board. The AVAB 40-3 was a flexible and compact solution that was popular with touring companies.
- 1977 The first computer-based console (2000) was presented. It was a preset-oriented board with two monitors, remote focusing and a pin-matrix backup. A year later they presented the touring version, '2001', in a small Zero Haliburton case. It was the first ultracompact 96-channel touring board, with remote control and incorporated displays as well as support for an external monitor. The 2001 was popular with touring theatre companies but was also used at rock venues for artists such as Supertramp, Rod Stewart, Pink Floyd.
- 1981 The Viking was launched. A high-end 1000-channel system with voice synthesis that can 'read' cue texts to the operator, it also had an acoustic modem for remote servicing, which was spectacular at the time. The wheels used for speeding up timed fades in the double playbacks were fitted with servo brakes to provide 'tactile feedback' to the operator's fingers, an expensive and complicated but elegant solution to the problem of returning to the 'original' rate of a fade after speeding up or slowing down with rate wheels.
- 1982–1985 Smaller systems were released called 201, 202 and 211, of which the 240-channel compact 202 board became popular with European touring companies.
- 1986 The Expert line was introduced, one of the first larger (512-channel) theatre consoles with a full MIDI implementation, ASCII Light Cues and an on-line help manual. The line consisted of the Expert, mini Expert and Expert Junior.
- 1993 The VLC Safari software line replaced most earlier systems. It is a PC-based object-oriented software for large theatre venues, upgradeable from 32 to 6000 channels with support for moving lights, effects, time code, MIDI, CD-ROM control, serial data such as RS232 and Ethernet networking among other things. The console line consists of the Lynx, Panther and Tiger.
- 1996 Presto, a compact preset-oriented 160-channel theatre board for smaller venues, with support for scrollers and moving lights, was introduced.

Avolites (UK)

Around 1975 a group of touring concert lighting electricians saw the need for something other than the theatre three-scene boards that were being used at the time. Everyday touring was hard on the boards, and they would often start falling apart after some time. Also concert lighting required a board with blocks of memory faders and flash buttons for manual improvisations. Ian Wally, Murray Thomas and Paul Ollett decided to try making more tour-worthy dimmers and boards.

By 1977 they were successful enough to go into manufacturing full time. They made dimmers and analogue pin-matrix mastering boards that were reliable and robust enough to become a standard in the touring industry.

- 1982 Avolites presented the first 180-channel QM500, which brought the 'live' concert desks from analogue pin-matrix memories to computer-assisted memories.
- 1984 The range was expanded with the first Rolacue, which implemented a 'roller' above the master faders instead of displays, and could change memory bank (page) for the masters when 'rolled'. The name of each memory can be written directly on the roll. The idea for the roll was to lower the cost of the boards (displays were very expensive at the time) and was popular with many operators, with its obvious functionality.
- 1985 Richard Salzedo joined the company, and, coming from the theatre world, decided to add theatre style editing from a keypad, and a rate playback to the QM500 in 1987.
- 1988 A full 'theatre version' of the QM without the channel faders was presented: QM TD (as in Theatre Desk). Around this time their boards were fitted with 3.5″ disk drives and an SMPTE Time Code option for running cues in a playback. Originally, the idea was to incorporate projections into a show 'in a better way than a bleep on a tape'.
- 1991 The company presented the QM Diamond I, based on the QM500 panels with the TD's digital engine under the hood. The channel faders were back, along with the fast response times for flash keys.
- 1992 Seeing that DMX512 moving lights and scrollers were clearly coming to stay, the company presented the Rolacue Sapphire, designed to control these as well as generic lights. This was one of the first boards to address moving instruments by patching personality files for each fixture. Once a Golden Scan (for example) was patched, all features of that specific light were automatically mapped to the controls of the board. Preset focus positions were introduced to simplify programming of moving lights.
- 1993 QM Diamond II was presented as the state-of-the-art touring console, with four times the capacity of a Sapphire, and the same philosophy or integrating moving lights and generic lights in the same board.

- 1994 Avolites presented the Pearl (30-channel), in the Rollacue mould but half the size. Also this year a new interface for programming moving lights was presented for the Sapphire, Pearl and Diamond boards: fixtures are calibrated to four corner points on the stage, which are mapped to a digitizer pad, the digitizer pen is then used to position an instrument(s) to any position within this area, including live follow-spot operations. The digitizer can also be used for colour mixing and for creating effects.
- 1996 The 120-channel QM Diamond III was launched to fill a gap between the Sapphire and the Diamond II.

Celco (UK)

Celco was founded around 1981, aiming at the 'live' market for concerts, touring and clubs. The main concert systems at the time were either the Avolite pin-matrix mastering boards or manual three-scene preset boards. The company wanted to bring the technology of theatre boards like the MMS into rock desks, replacing the pin matrix with memories.

- 1981 Celco presented the 30–90-channel Gamma line. The Gamma boards were channel fader boards with submasters as main playbacks. Memories could be stored for the submasters in banks, called 'pages', and there were eight character LED displays over each master to display the memory loaded to it. There was a sequence master to which a stack of memories could be loaded and run as an effect loop. Even though the concept was revolutionary compared to pin-matrix mastering, it was slow to catch on, partly because many designers weren't thinking beyond the need for 24 fixed submasters at the time.
- 1984 The Gamma boards were replaced by the Series II; the main difference was that memories could be edited (!) and the colour of the board was changed from brown to black (apparently appealing more to a somewhat design-sensitive market). The Series II became very popular and is probably one of the most widely-used rock boards to this day.
- 1988 The '88' line was launched revamping the Gamma boards into modern polycarbonate panels. Each channel fader had a 'limiting' pot, that could scale down the output of that channel. This feature appealed greatly to television since it allowed complete control over all board channels in a straightforward way.
- 1986 The board line was expanded with the Celco Gold, a luxurious hardware repackaging of the 90-channel board which helped Celco make the final break into the high-end concert market with acts like the Rolling Stones and David Bowie.

- 1989 The whole 88 range was improved with smart card memory storage, DMX outputs and improved functionality. This was the 30, 60, 90 and Gold Mayor line. The same year Panorama was presented, a moving lights board with analogue outputs, addressing the growing popularity of moving mirrors in concert lighting.
- 1991 The 96-channel Navigator was introduced, with the last action approach of a memory board with a single output scene and several group masters addressing that same 'stage door'. The Navigator is one of Celco's biggest selling products. The Pathfinder followed in 1992.
- 1993 The immense Aviator was launched, a last action rock desk for up to 1000 channels (!), and the Navigator last action approach of 'group faders in a single-scene channel window'. The space age-designed system involved several special patents for new kinds of faders among other things.
- 1995 The Explorer was launched, a more regular rock board for smaller venues with facilities for automated playback of cues.
- 1996 Celco presented Ventura, a 1000-channel moving lights hybrid for the live and touring market where up to 100 moving fixtures are controlled simultaneously along with conventional lights.

Compulite (Israel)

In 1979 lighting designer Dan Redler and electronics engineer Fred Senator formed a company that set out to manufacture theatre and television lightboards in an Israeli garage. The company focused on microprocessor technology from the start, and grew fairly quickly into a complete R&D department, partly due to support from the Israeli government which favours high tech companies.

- 1980 A whole line of entertainment consoles were launched under names like Mini and Micron. These were primarily sold in Europe, especially in Holland.
- 1983 A high-end theatre console for conventional lights for up to 1000 channels was launched, called the Ovation. The Ovation line has been constantly updated during the years, and is still their top-of-the-line theatre console. A smaller version called the Applause was launched shortly after.
- During the late 1980s the company cooperated with the French company Cameleon, that were manufacturing a high-end moving mirror for theatre applications. A dedicated moving lights board called the Telescan was manufactured. The company was gathering a lot of experience about controlling moving lights which resulted in the Animator a few years later.

- 1990 The Animator was launched, which was a pure moving lights board with support for several proprietary protocols from moving lights manufacturers such as High End, Summa and Cameleon. The Animator could control 72 moving units along with conventional lights, which made it very popular for moving lights applications both in Europe and in the United States. It is still manufactured as part of the moving lights line of boards and today is called the Animator Plus, with a capacity for up to 96 moving lights.
- 1995 A new family of boards was launched. The Photon, which is a conventional lightboard for up to 512 channels and 48 scrollers, and the Spark, which is a moving lights console for 24 or more moving lights along with 48 scrollers and up to 512 channels of conventional lights.
- 1996 The Sabre was launched, a console for up to 192 moving lights with capacity for conventional lights in the spirit of the Animator but with more extensive hardware, Ethernet, internal hard disk drive. There is still support for proprietary moving protocols, as in the Animator series.

ETC (US)

In 1975 Fred Foster, a technical theatre student at UW-Madison, started a company together with his brother, Bill, and a few friends who shared a common interest in theatre, technology and sailing. They wanted to create a processor-based lightboard in the $5000 range that could compete with the functionality of the $250,000 systems like the LS-8.

- 1978 The first console (Mega-Q) was manufactured for Colortran; they also created the Channeltrack for a theme park. In 1982 they created a product for a theme park that they were free to market afterwards. Colortran wasn't interested so they went into business for themselves.
- 1983 Their 125-channel Concept was introduced to compete with the Kliegl Performer, followed by their 125-channel Idea board with 12 submasters in 1985.
- 1985 The 100-channel Vision was produced, which was a super-compact lightboard with two playbacks, a disk drive and no submasters, which sold around 400 units at $4000 list price, quite a success. Concept, Idea and Vision were also sold to Arri Europe and presented there as the Arri Imagination, Imagine and Mirage.
- 1987 The company's Expression line for up to 500 channels was started, which was a continuation of their earlier preset-oriented boards with double playbacks, more submasters, and improved functionality. The preset orientation of these boards (Impression, Expression and Insight) has been popular in theatre, industrial shows and the theme parks that were among ETC's first customers.

- 1992 Ann Valentino (former Strand R&D) joined ETC and together they set out to make a worthy replacement for the original tracking Light Palette, aiming at Broadway. The result was the Obsession line, a tracking console true to the first Light Palette in essential features but with improved features, an improved effects package, time code support, networking, smart on-board displays, improved command line syntax and distinct hardware.
- 1996 ETC's preset-oriented line was enhanced with the Express line, which endorses most of the functionality in the Expression line, including, among other things, Ethernet networking, MIDI, SMPTE, digitizer option for moving lights and dimmer feedback for venues from 24 to 250 channels.

Flying Pig Systems (UK)

Around 1991 Nick Archdale, a lighting designer with a hardware engineering background who had designed and programmed endless series of eight-hour dance shows with moving lights on his own DMX console (DLD 6502), founded Flying Pig Systems together with Tom Thorne and Nils Thorjussen. The three of them travelled around the United States visiting people in the business, trying to conjure up what kind of a moving lights system they could come up with that would solve the problems Nick had run into trying to create interesting dance marathons with DMX-controlled moving lights in almost no programming time.

- 1992 The company launched the Wholehog, a last action console designed to control moving lights for touring and concerts. Wholehog was one of the first dedicated DMX moving light consoles that approached the problems of programming with 'personalities' for moving instruments, preselection 'palettes' and 'focus presets' that could be combined to speed up programming. The Wholehog was used early on by the Rolling Stones, Pink Floyd, Sting, Grateful Dead and many other larger acts. At that time there were almost no alternatives for controlling moving lights by DMX since Varilite and Morpheus systems were proprietary systems.
- 1995 The improved Wholehog II with added theatrical functionality was produced. As a hardware solution to the problem of wanting many function keys without getting a 'cluttered' hardware, two touch screens which double as monitors were introduced. This made the product both compact and user friendly, allowing each 'touch key' to be labelled with text by the user.

  Cues can be stored with individual fade times for every single channel or attribute, and stacked in different cue lists that can be played back in either of the eight parallel playbacks. All eight playbacks can be linked to operate from a single GO button, and they can control light intensities selectively as LTP or HTP. There is an effects package designed to automate any kind of mundane, repetitive moving lights programming.

The Wholehog is a moving lights board with support for conventional lights, providing a concept merging the qualities of 'playing' and 'playback' boards.

Strand Lighting (UK)

Strand (1914) has been involved in a multitude of innovative theatre installations from the days of Grand Master resistance switchboards and clutch-operated transformer dimmers, when designer Frederick Bentham modified a theatre organ into the Light Console. Several other control solutions were invented, some of which have been mentioned at the beginning of this book. This is a summary of the company's contributions to modern lighting control systems from the point where the MMS (Modular Memory System) was introduced.

- 1974 Strand installed the first MMS, which was a hardwired memory console competing with the Thorn Q-File at a much lower price and with improved theatre features. The MMS was modular, allowing a system to be tailored to requirements and budget. The MMS was the first memory board sold on a large scale, introducing the channel wheel and calculator style addition of channels and groups to set levels (direct entry syntax). There was a mimic panel with direct keys for all channels and there were two timed playbacks. MMS systems eventually pushed the Q-File off the market, and were sold worldwide, making it one of the dominating memory systems well into 1980.
- 1977 The Lightboard was presented. A 1000-channel console with integrated control for moving lights (proprietary) that was designed to Richard Pilbrow's specification for the National Theatre in London. Lightboard was an impressive ($250,000) system with extensive control possibilities. The system was the first last action board with multiple playbacks that had group faders, double screens and a double floppy disk station. The Lightboard was designed specifically to allow the board to be 'played'; there were eight different GO keys for each playback!
- 1980 The 1000-channel Galaxy replaced both the MMS and the Lightboard, with the MMS modularity and the lighting approach of the Lightboard. The Galaxy sold worldwide even though at the time Strand was selling the Light Palette as well in Europe. Two successful

smaller systems with the technology of the Galaxy were presented shortly after: the 365-channel Gemini and the 120-channel Tempus M24.

- 1993 The Tempus M24 was replaced by the GSX and LBX line of consoles with 'channel to fader' functionality, a new hardware approach and modular software.
- 1994 The 400 and 500 line was presented, running GeniusPlus modular software that can provide both group fading or tracking functionality selectable by the user, and with softaware modules that support scrollers, moving lights, networking, MIDI, time code and serial data. The Gemini was replaced by this line of consoles.

Transtechnik (Germany)

Siemens is one of the oldest companies involved in lighting. They manufactured their own line of memory consoles for a while, then Transtechnik was subcontracted to design new consoles up to the point where Siemens acquired ADB and their line of consoles. At this point Transtechnik continued under their own name.

At the beginning of the 1980s, Siemens presented a high-end theatre board called the Sitralux B40, based on a Siemens minicomputer. This system was one of the first systems to permit a single time per channel in a cue playback. The functionality of the B40 was especially adapted for larger theatres, and the system was popular in Germany.

- 1983 A system for television based on the B40, called the K40, was developed by a subcontracted company called Transtechnik, that had been around since 1965, catering for the German television lighting industry with customized control systems, and also manufacturing electrical test equipment and power converters.
- 1987 Siemens contracted Transtechnik to develop a 240-channel touring board, called the T40, in the spirit of the B40. This was the last cooperation between Transtechnik and Siemens, due to the fact that Siemens acquired ADB around that time. From this point Transtechnik went into business for themselves manufacturing both theatre and television controls.
- 1990 The T90-M, for up to 999 channels, was launched, one of the first theatre boards using Ethernet to synchronize a backup system. The T90 adapted most of the concepts of the Sitralux B40. The M stood for modular software, because different software modules for effects and other applications could be added to the same hardware platform.
- 1993 The 120-channel T40 was upgraded, with a new engine and the software features of the T90-M, to T40-M, capable of running most of

the software features of the larger board, including controlling up to 999 channels.

- 1994 The 120-channel T20-M was launched, a small television and touring version of the T40M with only ten submasters, but capable of running most of the software features of the larger boards and controlling up to 999 channels.
- 1995 Prisma was launched, which was the T90-M in a new hardware platform with controls for moving lights, retaining compatibility with all older and smaller boards.
- 1996 The Focus was launched, which was the moving lights version of the T40-M. All boards share the same software family and are run in a similar hardware platform, which means they share the same user interface, parts are interchangeable and shows are compatible.

US market: a general background

At the beginning of memory lighting control, the US market was catered for by European products like the Q-File (see Chapter 1), but computer technology advances and local preferences led to a market of nationally developed products. Some of these early companies are now defunct.

- 1973 Steve Skirpan, the manufacturer of a competing product (Autocue), filed a patent suit concerning the use of CRTs with computerized theatre lightboards which stopped the LS8 (by EDI) from going on tour with 'Chorus Line'. Wally Russel at Strand contacted David Cunningham, a physicist and part time actor who had been working for Van Beuren (a US engineering company that had designed Strand's earlier Memo-Q and Mini-Q II systems). David joined Strand to create a lightboard that could bring 'Chorus Line' on tour with the functionality of the LS8. The splendid result was the Multi-Q.

  Multi-Q was a 128-channel computerized memory system with channel faders for plotting cues, and double playbacks. There was concern from the lighting designer about the artistic qualities of playing back memories as automatic fades. A split fader was mounted on the fly and would turn out to be the control mainly used. Only two longer timed fades were used in that show, one of 90 seconds going to 'Paul's monologue' and one of 45 seconds 'Going to Cathy's dance'.

  Thanks to the popularity of the musical and the unrivalled functionality of the system, together with a price around $50,000 (half that of the LS-8), the MultiQ swept the US market (which at the time meant around ten systems a year).
- 1977 Strand Century came out with Micro-Q, a smaller 96-channel version of the Multi-Q, at half the price. At the same time Gordon Pearlman

and Steve Carlson had gone from EDI (which manufactured the LS-8) to Kliegl to create a board that could compete with the Multi-Q – the Kliegl Performance, a versatile board in the spirit of the Q-File with miniature manual channel faders that could function as a backup with a separate power unit and an optional VDU. Kliegl enjoyed great success when they produced the touring version of the Performance, the Kliegl Performer. EDI continues manufacturing preset-oriented boards and Gordon Pearlman has continued manufacturing controls. A PC-based lighting console software for up to 3000 channels was launched in 1996 through ROSCO.

- 1980 Strand released the Light Palette (LP), which was the first tracking last action board and became very popular with sequential productions (see Chapter 1). The success of the LP was followed by a series of LP boards, the Mini Palette, the Mini Light Palette, LP2 and LP3, which were improved versions of the original LP. David Cunningham left Strand in 1980 and joined Colortran to design the Prestige line of boards, which were based on a PC hardware platform. Afer this he moved on to ETC and has recently designed the Source Four lantern concept. After the LP90, R&D was moved to Strand in England where the tracking functionality of the Light Palette remains a user option in the software of their modern consoles.

Bibliography

Anderton, Craig (1986) *Midi for Musicians*. A basic introduction to MIDI from a musical perspective. ISBN 0-8256-1050-8

Bellard, F. Willard (1967) *Lighting the Stage*. Harper & Row. A thorough but aging book on lighting techniques for the theatre lighting designer. ISBN 0-8102-0040-6

Bentham, Frederick (1968–1980) *The Art of Stage Lighting*. Pitman. A book with a lot of fascinating details about very early lighting controls, most of which were designed by the author during his 40 years with Strand Lighting.

Bergman, Gösta M. (1971) *Lighting in the Theatre*. Rowman and Littlefield, New Jersey. An excellent book about antique lighting techniques written for The Stockholm Studies in Theatrical History. ISBN 0-87471-602-0

Cunningham, Glen (1993) *Stage Lighting Revealed*. Better Way Books. A book on stage lighting that is refreshingly up to date. ISBN 1-55870-290-3

Huntington, John (1994) *Control Systems for Live Entertainment*. Focal Press. A technically very thorough book about communication protocols with connection examples for show control systems and a chapter with explanations on the inner workings of different lighting protocols.

Parker, W. Oren and Smith, K. Harvey (1979) *Scene Design and Stage Lighting*. A classic on theatrical productions and lighting techniques. ISBN 0-240-51334-7

Pilbrow, Richard (1979–1986) *Stage Lighting*. Cassell. A fine book covering the art of lighting and work of lighting designers.

Rosenthal, Jane (1979) *The Magic of Light*. A fine book on lighting techniques and outdoor lighting by one of the true pioneering lighting designers.

Index